9 ROUTES TO SUCCESS
for Students

9 ROUTES TO SUCCESS
for Students

Robert K. Throop

Alan Gelb

MILADY
THOMSON LEARNING

Australia　Canada　Mexico　Singapore　Spain　United Kingdom　United States

9 ROUTES TO SUCCESS
for Students

Robert K. Throop
Alan Gelb

Milady President: Susan L. Simpfenderfer	Executive Editor: Marlene McHugh Pratt	Acquisitions Editor: Pamela B. Lappies
Developmental Editor: Judy Roberts	Executive Production Manager: Wendy A. Troeger	Production Editor: Eileen M. Clawson
Executive Marketing Manager: Donna J. Lewis	Channel Manager: Nigar Hale	Cover Design: TDB Publishing Services

COPYRIGHT © 2001 by Milady, an imprint of Delmar, a division of Thomson Learning, Inc.
Thomson Learning ™ is a trademark used herein under license.

Printed in the United States of America
1 2 3 4 5 XXX 05 04 03 02 01 00

For more information contact Milady,
3 Columbia Circle, PO Box 15015,
Albany, NY 12212-5015

Or find us on the World Wide Web at http://www.milady.com

For permission to use material from this text or product, contact us by
Tel (800) 730-2214
Fax (800) 730-2215
www.thomsonrights.com

ISBN 1-56253-677-X

ALL RIGHTS RESERVED. No part of this work covered by the copyright hereon may be reproduced or used in any form or by any means—graphic, electronic, or mechanical, including photocopying, recording, taping, Web distribution, or information storage and retrieval systems—without written permission of the publisher.

NOTICE TO THE READER

Publisher does not warrant or guarantee any of the products described herein or perform any independent analysis in connection with any of the product information contained herein. Publisher does not assume, and expressly disclaims, any obligation to obtain and include information other than that provided to it by the manufacturer.

The reader is expressly warned to consider and adopt all safety precautions that might be indicated by the activities herein and to avoid all potential hazards. By following the instructions contained herein, the reader willingly assumes all risks in connection with such instructions.

The Publisher makes no representation or warranties of any kind, including but not limited to, the warranties of fitness for particular purpose or merchantability, nor are any such representations implied with respect to the material set forth herein, and the publisher takes no responsibility with respect to such material. The publisher shall not be liable for any special, consequential, or exemplary damages resulting, in whole or part, from the readers' use of, or reliance upon, this material.

CONTENTS

ROUTE ONE
In Self We Trust:
The Power of Self-Belief — 1

ROUTE TWO
The Goal Zone:
Goal Setting...Goal Keeping — 17

ROUTE THREE
It's All in the Mind
Improving Your Intellectual Potential — 35

ROUTE FOUR
The Whole You:
Head to Toe — 55

ROUTE FIVE
Welcome to the World:
How Do You Fit In? — 75

ROUTE SIX
Get a Grip:
Harmony with Others and within Yourself — 95

ROUTE SEVEN
Where Did the Time Go?
Staying on Top of Your Schedule 115

ROUTE EIGHT
Show Me the Money
(And Then What Do I Do with It?) 137

ROUTE NINE
Never Chew Gum on an Interview and
Other Career Things You Should Know 159

A LETTER TO THE STUDENTS

Self-belief is the cornerstone of success in all personal, educational, and professional accomplishments. In order to succeed, you must deal with personal and economic problems and make a commitment to work to achieve your goals. A solid sense of who you are and who you will become is the springboard for overcoming obstacles and succeeding in school and all other areas of life.

9 Routes to Success for Students is designed to help you take control and improve your self-belief. The text provides a blend of concepts and applications to help you discover your emotional, intellectual, and social potential. Through a process of learning and self-examination, you will discover your values, increase your commitment to personal goals, and challenge yourself to grow and learn.

As you grow and change, your vision of a compelling future and your goals will also change. We hope you have great success in your schooling and in your career, and take these skills with you to serve you all your life.

The Publisher

ACKNOWLEDGMENTS

The authors and the publisher wish to express their gratitude to the following reviewers for their many helpful suggestions:

Lisha Barnes
    Olympian University of Cosmetology
    Alamogordo, NM

Madeline Udod
    Farmingdale, NY

Peggy Johnston
    Champion Institute of Cosmetology
    Palm Springs, CA

Linda Rice
    Grace College of Cosmetology
    Middleburg Hts, OH

Karen Wackerman
    Kar-Che, The Professional Career Center
    Phoenix, AZ

Laurol Boik
    Hastings Beauty School, Inc.
    Hastings, MN

Cindi Gill
    Body Business School of Massage
    Durant, OK

Pam Garrison
    Vincennes Beauty College
    Vincennes, IN

Jeffrey Pippitt
    Western Nebraska Community College
    Sidney, NE

Kathy Troup
    Bayshire Beauty Academy
    Bay City, MI

Cheryl McDonald
    Solano Community College
    Pleasanton, CA

John Halal
    Honors Beauty College, Inc.
    Indianapolis, IN

ROUTE ONE

IN SELF WE TRUST: THE POWER OF SELF-BELIEF

KEY TERMS

self-validation
values
beliefs
self-fulfilling prophecy
positive self-talk

Do you often find yourself envying those confident people who can walk into a roomful of strangers and not look for somewhere to hide? Those who can speak up in a classroom discussion and let their opinions be heard? Those who can acknowledge when they don't know something and ask for the help that they need?

Such people are not "super" people. They are simply people who are further along on the journey toward **self-validation** than most people. Let's take a moment and think about the word "validation." Many of you think of "validation" as having a parking ticket stamped at a shopping mall. This kind of validation serves as proof or confirmation that you were actually where you said you were, and the payoff is either free parking or some kind of discount. Validation in the larger sense also has to do with a kind of proof or confirmation, but in this case not so much as *where* we were as *who* we are.

Many people grow up seeking validation because they have never been able to form a truly positive self-image. They may feel that they were neglected by family, peers, and teachers and were deprived of the attention and rewards they needed.

People who continue to search for validation throughout their lives often look for that validation in the accumulation of material goods that are, in the minds of many, synonymous with success. If we have a grand home, a sportscar, a gold watch, a diamond necklace, we are "validated" in the most obvious way possible. Everyone can see that we are noticeable and successful (at least, financially successful). But seeking validation through material goods may lead us to feel empty in the long run. The only real validation that is meaningful in the long run is self-validation. It is very important for each and every individual to arrive at a place of self-validation; but to do so, we must first be clear about what success actually is and how it relates to values.

WHAT IS SUCCESS ANYWAY?

As mentioned before, in our society, success is most often equated with riches, fame, and glamor. Many people dedicate their lives to pursuing this formula of success, at the expense of personal relationships, health, and genuine happiness. But there is a great deal more to success than obtaining material goods, awards, first-class seats, and the like. There are also intangible rewards: being the kind of person whom other people want to be around; being able to handle the pitfalls that inevitably come with success; and being rounded in the sense that you enjoy not only material things, but the spiritual, natural, and emotional parts of life as well.

Think about it, and you'll realize that we all know someone whom we regard as a "successful" human being, even if that person is not someone who has a lot of money to throw around. The dedicated teacher wearing the same three outfits day after day who knows how to inspire a classroom full of kids. The overworked nurse who takes the time to help your family understand a little more about a health crisis. The low-paid day-care worker who shows up every day with a smile because she loves her work. Golf champion Chi Chi Rodriguez once said, "The most successful human being I know is my dad and he never had anything financially."

Success, then, is not directly connected to a bank balance. Successful people are those who are fulfilled emotionally, intellectually, socially, and physically. They see life not as an arena in which to "win," with million-dollar salaries, bonuses, and endorsements, but as a journey that has countless dimensions, paths, pitfalls, and heights—all of which will be explored at some time or another.

EXERCISE 1-1 Who Are You?

Successful people usually have a clear sense of who they are and what they want out of life. Take a few minutes to think about yourself and your life. Then answer the questions below:

1. I like:

   a. _____

   b. _____

   c. _____

2. I appreciate:

   a. _____

   b. _____

   c. _____

3. I am good at:

   a. _____

   b. _____

   c. _____

4. Someday I would like to:

   a. _____

   b. _____

   c. _____

THE VALUE OF VALUES

Albert Einstein, recently named in the *Time Magazine* millennium poll as the greatest human being of the century, had this to say on the subject of success: "Try not to become a man of success but rather try to become a man of values." What are **values**, where do you get them, and how do you keep them? Let's have a look:

Values are all your deepest feelings and thoughts that, put together, make up the code by which you live your life. Values are made up of three parts: (1) what you think, (2) how you feel, and (3) how you act, based on those thoughts and feelings. For example, if honesty is a value you hold dearly, then surely you *think* that telling a lie is wrong. What's more, if someone you trust lies to you, you *feel* betrayed. When you make a mistake, you *act* by owning up to it, rather than lying about it. Like most other things in life, however, sticking to our values may not be absolute; even though we may claim honesty as a value, most of us will, at one point or another, find ourselves in the position of feeling that we have to be dishonest (to protect someone's feelings, for instance).

Values are acquired along the way (and sometimes, unfortunately, are dropped along the way) as we progress through life. We gather our values from our family, our friends, religious organizations, Boy Scouts, Girl Scouts, athletic teams, books, song lyrics...there are endless avenues toward value acquisition.

Despite the diversity of our nation's population, polls show that most Americans actually hold many values in common. As a people, we value honesty, ambition, responsibility, and broadmindedness. Peace, family security, and freedom are right up there. And let's not forget hard work. As famed hairdresser Vidal Sassoon once put it, "The only place that success comes before work is in the dictionary."

EXERCISE 1-2 What Do You Value?

Here is a list of 15 values arranged in alphabetical order. Study the list carefully. Then place a 1 next to the value most important to you, a 2 next to the value that is second in importance, and so on. The value that is least important to you should be ranked 15.

When you have completed ranking the values, check your list. Feel free to make changes. Take all the time you need so that the end result truly reflects your values.

Value	Rank	Value	Rank
Affectionate	_____	Honest	_____
Ambitious	_____	Logical	_____
Brave	_____	Neat	_____
Cheerful	_____	Obedient/respectful	_____
Competent/Capable	_____	Open-minded	_____
Courteous	_____	Responsible	_____
Forgiving	_____	Self-controlled/committed	_____
Helpful	_____		

A five-year study to determine what 120 of the nation's top artists, athletes, and scholars had in common came up with surprising results. Researcher Benjamin Bloom, professor of education at the University of Chicago, said, "We expected to find tales of great natural gifts. We didn't find that at all. Their mothers often said it was their other child who had the greater gift." The study concluded that the most important element common to these successful people was not talent but commitment (McNally, 1990).

EXERCISE 1-3 Reflecting on Your Values

Spend a few minutes thinking about how you ranked your values. Then answer the following questions:

1. Which of your value rankings are you satisfied with?

_____
_____
_____

2. Which of your value rankings are you dissatisfied with?

_____
_____
_____

3. Now go back to your value rankings and rank them again. Write your five most important values here:

_____
_____
_____

BELIEFS

Values are the deeply-held thoughts and feelings that order your life; **beliefs** are the specific attitudes that arise from your values. If, for instance, you value ambition, you are likely to hold the belief that a good education is an essential part of the scheme of a person's life. If you value responsibility, you're bound to be out there doing more than your share on school, church, and civic committees.

The Belief-Behavior Connection

Beliefs and behavior go hand in hand. We can go all the way back to Aesop, the ancient Greek writer of fables, to find examples of this. Think of Aesop's fable about the fox and the grapes. When the fox first spots the grapes, he thinks they look delicious. This belief influences his behavior, as he tries again and again to leap up and reach the fruit. When the grapes continue to elude him, he gives up and, in the process, changes his belief, convincing himself that the grapes are sour anyway and who needs them. These continual shifts in our beliefs shape our inner lives as we go on about our business, sometimes barely aware of them. But these beliefs, both negative and positive, have a strong influence on how we act.

Negative Beliefs. Remember the character of Eeyore, the mournful donkey in *Winnie the Pooh*? He was such a mess of negative beliefs that he could turn the most beautiful day into one with grey skies. Most of us have known an "Eeyore" personality or two, and some of us may answer to that description ourselves. Too many people carry around mental "garbage" that accumulates unnecessarily and weighs us down. This "garbage" can show itself in any number of random negative thoughts:

"I can't do algebra."
"I'm terrible at following instructions."
"Nobody ever notices me."
"Why bother?"

As uncomfortable and counterproductive as it is to carry around these negative thoughts, the situation will become even worse if these negative beliefs are allowed to go unchecked. The person who says she can't do algebra may, in fact, actually become incapable of doing algebra. The person who regards himself as terrible at following instructions may continually foul up routines. Why? Because these people become infected with what is known as a **self-fulfilling prophecy**: the belief that comes true simply because it is believed that it *will* come true. This is a phenomenon that is a first cousin to the "You're your own worst enemy" syndrome.

Positive Beliefs. The flip side of that same old negative song is a positive one. The good news—always sought after and cherished by those with a positive orientation—is that selffulfilling prophecies can be positive just as well as they can be negative. Indeed, positive self-fulfilling prophecies are crucial when it comes to inspiring action and change. Consider some of these positive pep talks:

"I can find the money to go to school."
"I can speak up when I'm nervous."
"I can learn to drive."
"Where there's a will, there's a way."

It has been shown that positive self-fulfilling prophecies can actually help people survive situations of extreme danger and stress, such as being adrift at sea or lost in the woods. Positive prophecies are not to be confused with wishful thinking, which is often an idle pursuit. Rather, positive prophecies are proactive, enabling beliefs that help you to focus on what you need to do to achieve your goals. They give you the self-confidence to persist and to prevail.

Other People's Beliefs. It is not just our own beliefs that influence the outcome of our pursuits. Most of us are influenced by the beliefs of others. When these beliefs are positive, the effects can be positive as well. The recent film *Music of the Heart* tells the real-life story of a dedicated music teacher, enacted by Meryl Streep, who turns her inner-city students into first-rate violinists out of the pure conviction that it can be done. Over time, a person's ability to make himself or herself available to other people who can positively influence them, or even *mentor* them, becomes an important factor in success.

On the other hand, having a parent, spouse, friend, or co-worker who spouts negative beliefs can be highly damaging to your own feelings about yourself—it is essential that you develop the ability to identify these "naysayers" and find some way of achieving some distance from them.

Victims and Nonvictims. The habitual carting around of mental "garbage" can ultimately lead one to become a full-fledged "victim." Victims operate from a position of weakness. Instead of making things happen in an active way, they allow things to happen to them in a passive way. Often, the things they allow to happen are bad things and this fuels their victimization and so develops a deadly cycle of low expectations and high failure rate.

Nonvictims, on the other hand, steer clear of negative feelings, understanding just how crippling they can be. Believing in their own abilities and powers, nonvictims often succeed where others fail. The Reverend Jesse Jackson, for example, grew up in poverty and went on to become a national leader. "My mother was a teenaged mother and her mother was a teenaged mother. With scholarships and other help, I managed to get an education. Success to me is being born in a poor or disadvantaged family and making something of yourself."

Nonvictims will often use simple behavioral modification techniques to keep at bay the kind of negative feelings to which we are all susceptible. One technique has to do with **positive self-talk**. Recognizing that the negative inner voice of gloom and doom needs to be silenced in order to succeed, the nonvictim talks back to that negative voice with a positive one. This positive self-talk has three main characteristics:

1. Positive self-talk consists of "I" statements. *I feel good about myself. I want to succeed. I know what I need to do to make it happen.* "I" statements such as these indicate that you have assumed the main role in your life and are in full, take-charge mode.

2. Positive self-talk uses the present tense. Using the present tense shows you are existing in the here and now, ready for action.

3. Positive self-talk is just that: positive, enthusiastic, upbeat, proactive. It focuses on *what is* rather than *what is not*.

Sometimes negative beliefs can be countered by another technique similar to the positive self-talk discussed above. The technique called "Stop Thought" is widely recommended by mental health professionals. When a person finds herself carried away by negative thoughts—let's say financial anxieties, for example—the "Stop Thought" technique may be just the solution needed. Here's how it works: Joan is driving along, on her way to a job interview at the Shear Images salon. She really needs this job. Her rent is two months overdue and if she doesn't start making some regular money, she may lose her apartment. "I'll be out on the street," Joan tells herself. "I won't have enough money for a deposit or an agent's fee. I'll never get back into the apartment market. I'll become a homeless person!" Suddenly, Joan gives herself a command: "STOP THOUGHT." It's a red light that Joan holds up in her mind. She knows herself well enough to identify when she's having a negative belief and she's simply not going to allow it. The negative thought is swiftly put aside and room is made for positive thoughts: "I am going to get this job because clearly I'm the right person for it." The negative thoughts and anxieties may reoccur, but for now, at this crucial time when she has to present herself in a favorable light on a job interview, the STOP THOUGHT is just the tool she needs.

EXERCISE 1-4 Use Positive Self-Talk

Each of the following is a negative self-belief. Rewrite each so that it becomes positive self-talk.

1. I'll never pass that exam. I missed too many classes.

   _____
   _____

2. Jeff must hate me since I treated him so badly yesterday.

   _____
   _____

3. That VCR is too hard to operate.

   _____
   _____

4. I'll never have enough money to buy a new car.

_____

_____

5. I'll be ____ years old before I get my certificate.

_____

_____

THE SEVEN BELIEFS OF SUCCESSFUL PEOPLE

Successful people have been shown to have much in common with each other. They are most likely to subscribe to a worldview that is marked by a positive orientation toward life. In his research on successful people, Anthony Robbins, author of *Unlimited Power* (1997), has uncovered seven common beliefs to which the majority of successful people subscribe:

1. **Everything happens for a reason and a purpose.** Life is made up of good and bad experiences. Instead of dwelling on the bad ones, successful people focus on the good ones and think in terms of future possibilities rather than present and past disappointments. A lost wallet with $50 in it is exactly that: a lost wallet with $50 in it. Your driver's license and credit cards can be replaced and the $50 will not make you or break you in the long run. You absorb the loss and move on, rather than telling yourself what a fool and a loser you are.

2. **There is no such thing as failure.** All actions have outcomes, some good, some bad. When a bad result occurs, it is no more than that: a bad result. Successful people can set aside the disappointment of a bad result and can look toward changing their actions and producing new and better results. A poor test score is disappointing but it must be taken in stride. Doing particularly well on the next test will even things out. You will survive.

3. **Whatever happens, take responsibility.** Blaming others for unsatisfactory outcomes is counterproductive. There is nothing to be learned from it. Successful people do not engage in blaming others when something goes wrong; rather, they assume responsibility and use the experience to grow on.

4. **It's not necessary to understand everything in order to use everything.** Successful people do not allow themselves to get bogged down in details. They learn what they need to know, generally by not being afraid to ask, and they disregard whatever is irrelevant. They see the "big picture" and exude an air of confidence even if they haven't mastered all the nuts and bolts of how something works.

5. **After yourself, people are your greatest resource.** Successful people recognize the need to build bridges to other people and the importance of maintaining those bridges. If they are working alongside a difficult person in an office or shop, let's say, they will find a way to coexist not only because they realize that this is important in the here and now, but because they know that down the road they may cross paths with this person again.

6. **Work is play.** No one succeeds by doing something they hate to do. Work should be exciting, challenging, interesting, and fun. (Which is not to say it can't be hard, frustrating, tiring and even exasperating at times.)

7. **There's no lasting success without commitment.** Successful people are not afraid to make commitments, be it to a job, a relationship or whatever. They don't "dilly-dally." They don't "hem and haw." They don't do half a job. They do a job and a half.

THE AMERICAN DREAM

John Paul DeJoria
Co-Founder and CEO of John Paul Mitchell Systems

The American Dream has become a reality for John Paul DeJoria, who sold Christmas cards and newspapers in East Los Angeles when he was nine years old, went through a period of homelessness during which he collected soda cans to make a few cents a day, and now heads up a hair care empire whose annual sales approach $200 million. When DeJoria got out of the Navy in 1964, he started in sales—first encyclopedias, then copy machines, insurance, and ultimately a sales job at Redken Laboratories, then the leading professional salon product company in the U.S. In 1980, he joined forces with Paul Mitchell, one of America's foremost hair designers, and together they introduced the revolutionary hair setting and styling process known as hair sculpting, bankrolling their new company with $700. "The American Dream is there," says DeJoria, who now runs 17 other businesses and is a noted philanthropist.

THE AMERICAN DREAM (Continued)

Madame C.J. Walker
The first African-American woman to become a millionaire.

The extraordinary woman known to history as Madame C.J. Walker was born Sarah Breedlove in 1867 on a Louisiana plantation, the daughter of former slaves who both died of yellow fever when Sarah was only seven. Married in 1882, at the age of 14, and widowed six years later, Sarah moved to St. Louis with her daughter. By 1905, Sarah had invented, patented, and brilliantly marketed hair and cosmetics products for women of color. She maintained that the formula was given to her in a dream. Using door-to-door marketing techniques with newsletters to her agents, she pioneered concepts that were later copied by many other successful companies and became a millionaire within seven years. In 1906, she married Charles Walker and was known thereafter as Madame C. J. Walker. After her death in 1919, Madame C. J. Walker's will stipulated that her company must always be headed by women, which it is today.

SELF-VALIDATION

At the beginning of this chapter, we talked about validation and how important it is to come to a place of self-validation. When an individual arrives at such a place, he or she experiences a real swell of confidence and internalizes a fundamental respect for his or her own abilities. Self-validation usually comes hand in hand with self-belief, a powerful resource that is there to be drawn on when bad things happen to a person, as they inevitably do. Self-validated people with a strong sense of self-belief know who they are and what they can accomplish. They know, most importantly, that they have value no matter what circumstances are imposed upon them.

EXERCISE 1-5 What's Your Self Belief?

Self-belief involves the way you think and feel about yourself. Use the following list of personality traits to describe your current self-belief.

ambitious	dumb	lonely	reserved
assertive	eager	loyal	responsible
bossy	fair	mature	sensitive
capable	funny	motivated	shy
caring	gloomy	neat	sincere
cheerful	goal-oriented	negative	sweet
confident	healthy	nervous	trusting
considerate	honest	open	unambitious
creative	humble	outgoing	understanding
daring	indecisive	passive	unhealthy
decisive	insensitive	polite	unmotivated
determined	intelligent	positive	warm
dishonest	irresponsible	quiet	

1. Current self-belief: I see myself as

_____
_____
_____
_____
_____

Now imagine yourself at a banquet. Your family, friends, fellow students, and co-workers are there to praise you. What qualities do you hope they talk about?

_____
_____
_____
_____
_____

2. Future self-belief: I hope to be

_____
_____
_____
_____
_____

Improving Your Self-Belief

The good news about self-validation and self-belief is that they are learned behaviors. We talked about positive self-talk and techniques like STOP THOUGHT, but this is also a good place to point out some other important avenues toward self-validation to keep in mind as you make your journey:

1. **Accept yourself.** Be kind to yourself—no one can be a better friend to you than you can be to yourself. Acknowledge your good qualities instead of berating yourself for any perceived shortcomings. Don't expect to be perfect—nobody is.

2. **Pay attention to yourself.** No one knows you better than you yourself...or at least that's the way it should be. Try to discover what gives you inner satisfaction and do the things that give you pleasure, even if, for now, those things can only be allotted mere moments in the course of a busy day. If cooking is your passport to peacefulness, take five minutes in the course of a day to make a delicious omelet. If gardening is what moves you, get out there in the dirt for a few minutes a day. If music is the tonic in your life, invest in a pair of headphones and turn a rattling commute into a time of peaceful transport.

3. **Use positive self-talk.** It's a language that can be learned. The good news is that it isn't difficult. It just takes practice, but, as you get into it, you'll find it so effective and even pleasurable that you won't mind practicing at all. Soon you'll see how satisfying it is to go through the day with your inner voice saying, *Good job* rather than spitting out, *Loser, Loser, Loser.*

4. **Don't be afraid to try new things.** An adventurous spirit adds a great deal of spice to life and can often lead you into areas of new and unexpected opportunities. Remember that there is no such thing as failure-only results. If you never try new things, it's unlikely you'll ever achieve your full potential.

5. **Remember that you are special.** Everyone is, in some way or another. No one has your particular set of capabilities and talents—these are as unique as a fingerprint. Your values, beliefs, and emotions, and the way you act upon them, make up the personality that is yours and yours alone.

OVERCOMING ALL OBSTACLES

While Sally was in cosmetology school, her husband was diagnosed with terminal cancer. Sally promised him that she would complete the program so he could see her graduate before he passed away. Making this dream a reality required the involvement of everyone in the school. Staff members helped make out a maximum time schedule, helped her obtain additional financial aid and even came in to open the school exclusively for her so she could get the clock hours she needed. Sally had to attend 48 hours per week, take care of her husband and their two children. It was a tall order, as tall as orders get, but with Sally's determination and the help of the entire team, she got the job done. Sally's husband died two weeks after she graduated. Sally is now a progressive, successful stylist and is supporting her two children.

REFERENCE

McNally, D. (1990). *Even eagles need a push: Learning to soar in a changing world* (p. 153). New York: Delacorte Press.

2 ROUTE TWO

THE GOAL ZONE: GOAL SETTING... GOAL-KEEPING

KEY TERMS

short-term goals
intermediate goals
long-term goals
measurable goals
procrastination
visualization

mastery approach
intrinsic motivation
extrinsic motivation
self-sabotage
perfectionist

Congratulations! If you're reading this now, that means you have already accomplished something that can be enormously hard to do: you have identified a goal. You know that you are interested in a career in styling. You have enrolled in a program that will enable you to achieve that goal. You're way ahead of those people who don't have a clue as to what they want to do with their lives. And you're way ahead of where you were a while back, when you weren't sure what you wanted to do with your life.

It is important, however, when you're involved in a pursuit, to continually go back to your goals to assess that where you are is where you set out to be. So let's have a look at the whole process of goal-setting and goal-keeping.

IDENTIFYING YOUR GOALS

Now that you've been congratulated on identifying your goal, let's back up a little. It's true that you are drawn to fashion. Were you the kind of kid who played with your sister's hair (or any head of hair you could get your hands on)? Maybe you were leafing through your mother's *Glamour* magazine when other kids were off watching cartoons. Barbie was more than a doll to you; she was an icon (and you don't mind saying so!).

Some part of you has always kept alive the dream of being involved in the world of beauty and fashion, even though there may have been factors arguing against this. Maybe your family felt you should become a teacher or a nurse. Maybe someone once told you that you had all the fashion sense of Drew Carey and you were crazy to even consider such a field. You might have doubted your own abilities and worried that you could never accomplish your goal.

But you prevailed. And here you are now. Keep in mind, however, that you may have only identified one type of goal—the professional goal—and that is merely part of a bigger picture.

GOAL-KEEPER

Monica, a fifteen-year-old high school vocational student, attended a goal-setting session her first week at her school. She posted these goals on her bedroom mirror and gave her instructor a copy of them. Periodically they were reviewed as she went about completing the program and once again at the time of her graduation. Monica continued to achieve her goals and at the end of her first two years as a practicing cosmetologist she had met most of her goals. Monica had her own salon at the age of 20, had two stylists working for her and had achieved a yearly income of $65,000—over $40,000 more than the average in her area. Now that's goal-keeping!

Goals: Challenging and Realistic

It would be a sad and dreary world if people weren't allowed to dream their dreams. Dreams can fuel our ambitions and even help point some people toward greatness. But dreams can also be destructively seductive, and there comes a time when we all have to step back from our dreams, examine them, and assess whether or not those dreams have any basis in reality. If, for example, you've always been drawn to the dream of being a colorist, your dream would probably never come true if you were color-blind. Similarly, if you've always dreamed of becoming a nail technician but, in reality, you're all thumbs, this is also a case of ignored reality. And when you ignore reality for too long, eventually you wind up having to pay a price.

Being realistic, however, doesn't necessarily mean giving up dreams that are long shots. Olympic heptathlon champion Jackie Joyner-Kersee, for instance, was plagued as a teenager by asthma; but, despite these difficulties, she continued to train and compete. Even so, however, your goals should have some realistic basis, taking into account your unique talents and abilities. This is not to say that they should not be challenging—a goal should be something to strive toward, that requires effort to achieve. Goals should not be so loaded with the potential for defeat that they become self-defeating almost from the start. You and trusted friends and advisors will be the judge of whether your goals make sense or not. If they do, strive on. If they don't, regroup and structure new goals that can be achieved with the same sense of satisfaction.

EXERCISE 2-1 What are Your Dreams?

Take a few minutes to write down what you've always dreamed of doing.

_____

_____

_____

Types of Goals

We mentioned above the *professional* goal—in your case, the goal of working in the field of styling. But there are other kinds of goals, each as important as the other. Together, they create a blueprint for the kind of life you want to live.

Personal Goals. *Personal goals* are those that relate to a person's private life. A personal goal may be to find someone with whom you can share your life. For many people, having children becomes an important goal. Goal-oriented people are likely to set up all kinds of personal goals for themselves: losing ten pounds, improving one's relationship with one's spouse, learning to play the piano, or bettering one's golf swing. Being aware of one's personal goals and working toward achieving them is a hallmark of those who achieve some real measure of satisfaction with their lives.

Educational Goals. The very fact that you're reading this book is proof that you are an individual with educational goals. For most people, educational goals are pursued within the structure of an established school curriculum: two-year college, four-year college, graduate school, professional school, and so on. These goals are validated by certificates, diplomas, and degrees that are designed to help you gain access to the professions of your choice. Educational goals can also be less structured and more personalized. You might want to improve your computer literacy by taking a few courses at a business school. You might want to pick up conversational Spanish by enrolling in an adult education course. You might want to create your own curriculum in a subject and read all you can about Greek mythology or African-American history or Shakespeare just because it interests you.

Professional Goals. The objectives you identify for your work life are your professional goals. Your professional goals might be related to the level of income you hope to achieve; they may be related to the degree of prestige you're looking to attain; they might have to do with the kind of security you're aiming for, as in tenure for a teacher; or they might be any combination of these factors and more. Your professional goals might also be more short-term in the beginning—getting your certification or license, let's say.

Community Goals. As the saying goes, "No man is an island…" or at least shouldn't be. Our lives are immeasurably enriched by our connections to other people in the community, and too many of us today tend to forget that. We become so involved in our personal goals (getting that time at the fitness club, for instance) and our professional goals (allowing our hard work to become workaholism) that we have nothing left for other people. As a result, communities suffer. There is no one to coach Little League and school meetings go sparsely attended. This is not the way things should be and so it is important for you to remember that you are one among many. Make time in your schedule for some community-oriented activity, whether it's working with needy people, giving kids the opportunity to pursue extracurricular activities, participating in a parent-teacher organization, getting involved in activities around church, synagogue or mosque, or working for the environment. Your working at community goals will not only improve your community, but it will leave you with a very special feeling of satisfaction.

The Long and the Short of It

Some goals, whether they be educational, professional, personal, or community, can be achieved in a matter of weeks or even less. Others might take a decade or more. When you're setting goals for yourself, it helps to figure out how much time you think you will need to achieve them. **Short-term goals** are those goals that take a year or less to achieve. **Intermediate-term goals** can usually be achieved in one to five years. **Long-term goals** may take you more than five years to accomplish.

Let's take, for example, the situation of someone who wants to become a real-estate broker. Her short-term goal would be to take a one-month course that will enable her to get a license that will allow her to work in a broker's office. Her intermediate-term goal would be to become a broker herself, which involves working for a documented three years in a broker's office. Her long-term goals might be to have her own office, which could take another few years of planning and saving to achieve.

Short-, intermediate-, and long-term goals often run together. In fact, it might be helpful to you as an individual to think of your long-term goals as a series of short and intermediate-term goals strung together. As you achieve them, you can check them off and measure your distance along the timeline toward your ultimate goal. For instance, earning an academic degree might be thought of as a long-term goal but each time you pass a course you've achieved your short-term goal. This way, your long-term goals never seem quite so overwhelming.

Six Rules for Stating Goals

Goal-setting can easily become day-dreaming if you don't go about making those goals concrete right from the start. The way to do this is by writing them down. Stating your goals helps you to focus in on them. Looking at them, formed in words on a page, convinces you that they exist, in the real here-and-now. In fact, studies have shown that people who write down their goals are far more likely to achieve them than those who do not.

There are several things to keep in mind when writing down your goals. These tips will help you make this process as meaningful and effective as it should be.

1. **Express your goals in positive language.** Writing down your goals should not become an opportunity for you to dump on yourself. Instead of writing, "I'm not going to cheat on another diet," try for "I'm going to achieve my desired weight." Similarly, instead of saying, "I'm not going to

get another D or F in English," opt for a positive phrasing, such as "I will get at least a C or maybe even a B in English." When writing down your goals, you'll find that positive language has the same beneficial effects as positive self-talk, which we referred to in the last chapter.

2. **Make your goals as specific as possible.** Instead of writing, "I am going to be rich," try "I am going to make $50,000 a year" (or $100,000, or whatever your goal actually is). Instead of writing, "I will see the world," start with, "I will travel to Cancun." Making goals specific helps you to focus your efforts on achieving those goals.

3. **Make your goals measurable.** Perhaps you grew up with the old-fashioned idea, drummed into you by your family, that saving some portion of your income is a good thing to do. But when you're thinking about taking that hard-earned vacation down to the Bahamas you've been dreaming about, you feel guilty. Why should you? All you have to do is have **measurable goals**. Tell yourself you're going to save $1,000 this year. Maybe that way there will be money left over for a vacation after you've appeased the Gods of Saving. Any goal becomes easier to face if there's a way of measuring it.

4. **Set yourself a deadline.** It's great to say you want to lose ten pounds...but not if you're planning to do it sometime, somewhere, somehow in the next twenty-five years. Get real with yourself. Tell yourself you're going to lose two pounds a week (that sounds conservative and healthy) and that it will take you six weeks to do it. (That gives you a week leeway in case you have a close encounter with a hot fudge sundae). Whatever your goal is, commit yourself to some kind of time frame. Decide when you will start and when it will be done. If an extension is needed, make believe you're the professor and give yourself a day or two to get it done—that's all!

5. **Have a variety of goals.** When it comes to goals, you want to keep a number of balls up in the air. Not only should your goals reflect a range of concerns, as we indicated above (professional, personal, educational, and community goals), but it is important to have a variety of goals so that if some fall by the wayside, there are others you can achieve. That way you can avoid feelings of failure that are absolutely counterproductive.

6. **Make your goals your own.** Your parents think you should be a teacher. Your partner thinks you should be a nurse. Your best friend thinks you were born to be a chef because you make great lasagna. But you know what you want to be: a stylist. So stay with it. Let your goal be just that: *your* goal. After all, it's your life and you're the one who's going to have to live it.

LIGHTS...CAMERA...ACTION!

Now that you've identified your goals, and understand the process and the requirements for informed goal-setting, it's time to act. You have a destination in mind; how do you get there? A written action plan will help you focus your efforts so that you can reach your goals without getting lost or mired along the way.

When you prepare your action plan, it's a good idea to plot out your long-term goals first. You want to start by having a strong sense of where you want to wind up. Let's say, for instance, that Alana wants to own her own salon. Her timetable is seven years. With that long-term goal in mind, she begins to set up a series of short- and intermediate-term goals that will help get her to her destination. (Think of it as a long bus trip with a number of transfers). First she has her short-term goal: complete the kind of training that you're now in, with anywhere between 800 and 2,400 hours of training, based on the state in which you're to be licensed. This goal typically takes between ten months and a year to complete. Alana now moves into the phase of her intermediate-term goal (the sort of goal that take between one and three years to complete), which is to become a manager of a salon, thus gaining the kind of across-the-board experience she feels she needs before owning her own salon. While she's doing this, she may take on other short-term goals, such as taking business and accounting courses, that she will hope to complete while she pursues her long-term goal. She will set for herself various personal goals that will help facilitate the goals described above. For instance, she will try to save 15 percent of her income each year toward the expense of starting a business. As an additional personal goal, she will give up smoking because she feels committed to being in the best health she can achieve and she feels that smoking in her own salon would be introducing an unattractive behavior she would rather deal with now.

Alana has created an action plan for a long-term goal. Essentially, the steps she took were:

1. Stating a long-term goal in specific terms and giving it a time frame.
2. Breaking down the goal into short-term goals, or steps, that will lead to achieving that long-term goal.
3. Paying close attention to the specific results of the short-term goals in order to monitor progress.
4. Setting deadlines for the short-term goals.

If you follow these steps for each of your intermediate- or long-term goals, you will have an action plan that will be central to achieving your goal. A plan for a short-term goal would eliminate Step 2 above. The plan should be written so that you can easily monitor your progress as you achieve your goals.

EXERCISE 2-2 What Are Your Goals?

Use the chart below to record your personal, educational, professional, and community goals. Remember to classify goals as either short-term (one year or less to accomplish), intermediate (one to five years), or long-term (more than five years to achieve). You may have more than one goal or no goals in a particular category.

Personal Goals

_____
_____
_____

Professional Goals

_____
_____
_____

Educational Goals

_____
_____
_____

Community Goals

_____
_____
_____

REACHING YOUR GOALS

An action plan plays a vital role in helping you to realize your goals, but it does not, by any means, offer fail-safe insurance against falling short of those goals. To make progress, you will have to work very hard, keep your goals clearly and firmly in sight, and persevere even when major problems present themselves. Some people have trouble getting started; others sag in the mid-game; still others stop just short of reaching their destination. Very few people continue calmly and without reversals on the complicated road of life. Most people, at one time or another, feel the need to supplement their own inner drive with some external boosting from family, friends, and support groups, informal or otherwise. Many of us have to come to terms with our feelings about success and failure before we can achieve success. Some of us lack the flexibility to change courses in mid-stream and adapt to new situations. All of us can benefit from some pointers provided by naturally optimistic people.

Taking the First Step

When astronaut Neil Armstrong landed on the moon, he talked of "taking one small step for man, one giant step for mankind." It was as dramatic a moment as history has ever provided and it was the capstone of a long-term goal that many initially thought was impossible. To get to the moon meant overcoming the tremendous pull of earth's gravity. More energy was used in lift-off and in the first few miles of travel than was used during the next few days to go a quarter of a million miles (Covey, 1989).

Lift-off and those first few miles are a big issue for earthbound folk as well when it comes to starting up a new project or identifying a new goal. Old habits often have as powerful a pull as gravity itself. Inertia, defined as a tendency to remain in a fixed condition without change, is a real danger and has dashed many a plan and wiped out many a goal. That little negative voice pipes up with questions like: *Why bother?* or *This isn't so bad anyway.* **Procrastination**, the fine art of putting off until tomorrow what you can do today, is a sure way to fail to reach one's goal. People who procrastinate usually convince themselves that they have a very "good" reason. They'll start their diet after their cousin's wedding (after all, you've got to eat some wedding cake, right?). They'll start saving a portion of their paycheck once they get that new 36-inch TV.

Postponing your goals, or the tasks that will take you toward the completion of your goals, does not make those goals or tasks any easier. In fact, it may make them harder to achieve because each time you procrastinate and postpone, chances are you're blowing that task out of proportion and the more you do it, the more baggage surrounds that task. The real reasons you are procrastinating may be because you're feeling shy, insecure, indecisive, or negative about yourself...none of which gets remedied by putting it off. Simply put, you feel you can't do something so you don't do it. And it doesn't get done....

To overcome procrastination, you have to change your beliefs and change your behavior. We've already discussed the powerful role that positive self-talk plays in improving your self-belief. If you are a procrastinator (and let's face it, so many of us are), now is the time for a healthy dose of that positive self-talk. For example, you might say something like the following to yourself: "I know I need to lose ten pounds and if I start right now, two weeks before my cousin's wedding, maybe I'll lose four or five pounds and look even better than I might have looked. I can do without sweets. I'll eat strawberries. I love strawberries. And I'll look great!" And there you have it—positive self-talk without the punishment.

Another technique that you might find useful is **visualization**. Visualization means imagining what it would be like to already have reached your goal. You *are* ten pounds lighter. Your clothes fit you more comfortably. People are remarking on how well you look, but, even more important, you can't get over how well you feel. Imagining the future in which you've achieved your goal can help propel us toward the completion of that goal, in order to create the kind of future we want. Visualizing your success provides the powerful mental boost to get the job done.

Getting Started: Here's How

If you're ready to own up to the fact that you're prone to procrastination, then here are some techniques for avoiding the procrastination trap.

- Set a deadline for getting started. It could be tomorrow; it could be a week from tomorrow. (Don't make it four months from tomorrow, because that's just another way for procrastination to show itself.) By focusing on a starting date and committing yourself to it, you'll discover the energy to begin.

- Make a list of small tasks to get you started. It will only take a minute or two to do so. Don't make lots of lists, because this, again, could be a mode of procrastination. Once you've made your list, undertake the first item on the list and check it off when it's completed. If it's that ten pounds you're after, the first item might be to throw away the cookies. Just doing that will use up a few calories!

- Doing anything in connection with completing your goal is better than doing nothing. If you have to write letters, let's say, and you hate writing letters and can't get started, at least you can look up the addresses and prepare the envelopes as a way of beginning. Again...it's better than doing nothing!

- Assign a short period of time during which you will work on your goal. This might work best for you on a daily basis. Five minutes a day, ten minutes a day...you name it. Then stick to it.

- Do the worst thing first. Sometimes tackling the hardest part of a job and getting it done can be the best route to getting the whole job done. After you've done the hard part, the rest will feel like gravy.

Any one of the above approaches, in combination with positive self-talk and visualization, will go far in helping you to achieve your goals.

EXERCISE 2-3 Prepare an Action Plan

1 Intermediate- or long-term goal: _____
   To be accomplished by: _____
   Step 1: _____
      Results needed: _____
      To be accomplished by: _____
   Step 2: _____
      Results needed: _____
      To be accomplished by: _____
   Step 3: _____
      Results needed: _____
      To be accomplished by: _____
   Step 4: _____
      Results needed: _____
      To be accomplished by: _____

2 Intermediate- or long-term goal: _____
   To be accomplished by: _____
   Step 1: _____
      Results needed: _____
      To be accomplished by: _____
   Step 2: _____
      Results needed: _____
      To be accomplished by: _____
   Step 3: _____
      Results needed: _____
      To be accomplished by: _____
   Step 4: _____
      Results needed: _____
      To be accomplished by: _____

3 Intermediate- or long-term goal: _____
   To be accomplished by: _____
   Step 1: _____
      Results needed: _____
      To be accomplished by: _____
   Step 2: _____
      Results needed: _____
      To be accomplished by: _____
   Step 3: _____
      Results needed: _____
      To be accomplished by: _____
   Step 4: _____
      Results needed: _____
      To be accomplished by: _____

Mastering the Mastery Approach

Chances are you've had the experience of getting off to a good start on some project and then found yourself getting bogged down and, before you knew it, giving up altogether. You experienced a burst of energy at the beginning, then you found yourself on a plateau where absolutely nothing was happening. You might have seen it happen with your Dad, too. He was all gung-ho about learning to play golf, and he was pretty good in the beginning; then he just stayed there, with that 20 handicap, never getting any better. But maybe your Dad got off that plateau after a while, with another burst of progress. Then something called mastery kicked in.

The secret of this **mastery approach** is to expect and accept hills, valleys, and plenty of plateaus in your route toward your goal. When this happens, don't give up! Hang in there and, with some of that positive self-talk you're getting so good at, tell yourself that plateauing is natural and you will, in time, make more progress if you just allow yourself the chance.

Motivating Yourself

It's all well and good to talk about hanging in there through the plateaus, but how do you actually *do* that? How do you motivate yourself to act in ways that will get you going again when you feel bottomed out?

The key word is *motivation*. Motivation is having the energy to work toward a goal. It is made up of either a simple or complex set of needs and incentives but, generally, motivation either comes from within or without...or sometimes from both places at the same time.

Motivation that comes from within you is called **intrinsic motivation**. Artists who feel blessed with a gift, athletes who have this great internal drive to run or jump or swim, politically-inclined people who have this instinct to reach out to other people, are operating out of an intrinsic motivation. They do what they do because they want to do it, they enjoy doing it, they feel compelled to do it, or they may even feel that they were put on this earth to do it.

Many people do not operate with that kind of intrinsic motivation but they do just fine anyway. They rely on **extrinsic motivation**, which is an outside reward for behavior. Our friend who's trying to lose ten pounds has been promised a night out dancing from her boyfriend if she reaches her goal. She loves to dance and that reward is the carrot at the end of the stick (although she's had her fill of carrots during this diet!).

Extrinsic motivation can be a powerful force for a while, but, over time, its value is liable to decrease. Rewards have to be continually sweetened and even then they may lose their magic charm altogether. The rewardee might well decide that she prefers chocolate eclairs to dancing. If, however, our friend decides that she really feels better about herself all around when she's ten pounds lighter, then she's operating from a place of intrinsic motivation and she's more likely to stay with her goal.

Psychologists have found that the most valuable form of extrinsic motivation is praise. Unlike other extrinsic rewards, praise helps fuel a person's self-esteem which, in turn, builds opportunities for intrinsic motivation. In any event, however, most people pursue their goals with some combination of intrinsic and extrinsic motivations. John, for instance, may enjoy learning how to use a computer (intrinsic) but he is also doing it to earn course credits (extrinsic).

If you are intrinsically motivated to achieve a goal, you run a good chance of actually reaching that goal. You enjoy working on your goal (even if it means lots of hard work), so you don't need to shop around for excuses to get you away from that work. If your intrinsic motivation is spotty, try using positive self-talk and visualization to keep up your energy level. Congratulate yourself as much as you can with regard to what you've managed to accomplish so far, stay off your back about your setbacks, and allow yourself to luxuriate in visions of what it will be like when you finally reach your goal.

If you need some extrinsic motivation to keep you going, you can do two things:

1. Set up a system of rewards for yourself. If you're dieting, allow yourself a small square of chocolate once a day or every other day. If you've been scrupulous about saving money, treat yourself to a little impulse buy now and then, even if it's just a bar of pretty soap or a scented candle. Just make sure that the reward does not become more important than doing the task you've set for yourself.

2. Enlist the support of family and friends. Why go it alone? If you can communicate what you hope to accomplish, the pride that others will take in seeing you reach your goals will provide a powerful motivation for you to persevere. Similarly, their love and support when you falter may well serve as the safety net to keep you from plummeting right back to the beginning: that place where all the inertia and procrastination awaits you.

EXERCISE 2-4 What Motivates You?

It's helpful to think about what motivates you to achieve your goals. Consider the three goals for which you prepared an action plan. What do you think will motivate you to accomplish these goals?

1 Goal 1:

Your intrinsic motivation: _____

_____

Sources of extrinsic motivation: _____

_____

2 Goal 2:

Your intrinsic motivation: _____

_____

Sources of extrinsic motivation: _____

_____

3 Goal 3:

Your intrinsic motivation: _____

_____

Sources of extrinsic motivation: _____

_____

Overcoming Fears

Perhaps you've always been a person who's been plagued by fears and insecurities. It was torture for you as a child to get up in class and give an oral report. Tests made your stomach turn over. Going for a job interview puts you in such a fog that you're likely to take wrong turns on your way to your appointment.

Being fearful is not something to brag about, but, by the same token, it is not something to be ashamed of either. It is a situation that many people share and it can be overcome. The first step toward overcoming fear is to understand what your fears are really about.

The two most important fears that can interfere with a person's reaching a sought-after goal are the fear of failure and the fear of success. Fear of failure is easy enough to understand. Nobody wants to be perceived as a loser. No one wants to be thought of as stupid, incompetent, or irresponsible. But it is actually our perception of failure that fuels our fear. Instead of seeing failure as the poor result of some effort we've made, or as some kind of temporary setback that, even if dire, can be largely remedied, we see failure as defeat and shame. If we keep in mind that everyone fails at times (even Michael Jordan didn't make his high school basketball team!) we can start to put failure into perspective. In fact, we can build on our setbacks and come up with important lessons to help lead us to the ultimate success that awaits us.

Fear of failure may be something you can easily relate to, but fear of success might not be in your particular vocabulary. In fact, however, fear of success plagues a great many people. People who fear success are seldom aware of it. Yet they put obstacles in the way of achieving their goals. Why? Because they're afraid that success will bring new situations and new responsibilities that they can't handle or that they feel they don't deserve. Or they may feel, without even being fully conscious of it, that their success might alter or even damage their relationship with a parent or a sibling or a partner. In fact, they probably are perfectly well-equipped to handle success and change, even if they go through periods of adjustment. However, this fear of success can be so powerful that it actually leads people to engage in what is known as **self-sabotage**, or ruining your chances so that you never get to the point of success.

If either type of fear has you in its grip—fear of failure or fear of success—it is best to remind yourself that fear is natural and that even though you may be experiencing fear, it should not keep you from striving for something.

Being Flexible

We've talked about the importance of being kind to yourself. Being flexible is, in fact, a way to treat yourself gently, kindly, and well. Life comes with a lot of change, and change is rarely expected or planned. People who don't adjust their goals accordingly are likely to run into problems. Today you want to be a stylist and you're in school to achieve this goal and that's terrific. Tomorrow, however, you could win a million dollars in a lottery or you could be in a car crash. You don't know what tomorrow brings, but you do know that if it brings change, good or bad, you have to go with the flow. Maybe one day you'll get back to your original goals, or maybe new goals will present themselves that are more in tune with your new situation. Goals and action plans are not carved in stone. When your situation changes, you will have to be flexible and change your goals and action plans to fit your new circumstances.

Being Less Than Perfect

If your goal is to be perfect, forget it. None of us are. Not even Martha Stewart. Keep in mind too, that people who are perfectionists often get bogged down in trying to reach their goals. They don't see The Big Picture and they focus obsessively on details. It's also a hard way to live. **Perfectionists** alienate other people in their quest for perfection, and they wind up suffering from their ruthless demands on themselves as well. They are always in a hurry but they never seem to quite get to where they want to be.

On the other hand, people who attain their goals tend to be more relaxed about themselves. They know they've worked hard and they're willing to reward themselves. They acknowledge that they are human and that all humans have faults. They make mistakes, but they own up to them and learn from them. They realize the importance not only of pleasing others, but of pleasing themselves. They are flexible and relaxed and open to new people and situations. These are the people who have the inner resources to really succeed over the long haul.

EXERCISE 2-5   Are You a Perfectionist?

Read the following pairs of sentences, and circle the letter of the sentence in each pair that is most like you.

1. a. I make mistakes occasionally.

    b. When I make a mistake, it's someone else's fault.

2. a. I do the best I can.

    b. It's hard, but I try.

3. a. My goals are pleasing to me.

    b. My goals are pleasing to my family and friends.

4. a. I take my time in getting things done.

    b. I'm always in a hurry to finish.

5. a. I'm open to sharing my feelings.

    b. I'd rather appear strong than show weakness.

If you circled three or more b's, you tend to be a perfectionist. Try to be easier on yourself!

The Importance of Hope

In recent studies, psychologists have determined what many people already suspect: that hope plays an important role in achieving success in life.

A study of 3,920 college freshmen showed that the level of hope at the start of school was a better predictor of their college grades than previous performance or standardized test scores or their high school grade-point average. Dr. Charles Snyder, a psychologist at the University of Kansas, says, "Students with high hopes set themselves higher goals and know how to work to attain them" (Goleman, 1991).

To Dr. Snyder, hope is more than just the feeling that everything will be okay. Rather, he defines hope as the belief that one has the will and the way to accomplish one's goals. In other words, people with commitment and self-belief are hopeful people.

People who are naturally hopeful are to be envied. Those of us who aren't, however, can learn more hopeful ways of thinking from those lucky people who are naturally hopeful. To imitate the mental habits of hopeful people, you can:

- turn to friends for help in achieving your goals
- use positive self-talk
- believe that things will get better
- be flexible enough to change your action plans when necessary
- be flexible enough to change your goals when necessary
- focus on the short-term goals you need to achieve in order to reach your long-term goal

When you have that hope as a tool and a comfort, you'll find there are all sorts of things you can manage to accomplish.

REFERENCES

Covey, S. R. (1989). *The seven habits of highly effective people* (p.46). New York: Simon & Schuster.

Goleman, D. (1991, December 24). Hope emerges as key success in life. *The New York Times,* pp. C1, C7.

ROUTE THREE 3

IT'S ALL IN THE MIND: IMPROVING YOUR INTELLECTUAL POTENTIAL

KEY TERMS

multiple intelligences
sensory memory
short-term memory
long-term memory
mnemonics
critical thinking

deductive reasoning
inductive reasoning
reactive responses
proactive responses
brainstorming

If you're one of those people who has never had an easy time with the school experience, you may already have it in mind that you're no "brain." Maybe teachers, family, or peers told you that you were "nice" or "sweet" or "funny" but you shouldn't plan on becoming a rocket scientist. These kinds of messages have left you feeling vulnerable on the self-esteem front. Perhaps you've even chosen your field *because you didn't think you could do any better.*

To all of this, we say "Think again"...with the emphasis on "Think." Most likely, you've got a perfectly good mind and now, as you set off on this new course, it's as good a time as any for you to use that mind to the fullest.

Studies have shown that all of us have far more brain power than we use. We can improve our ability to think and reason by tapping into some of that unused power. But first let's look at some interesting thoughts about intelligence itself.

THE THEORY OF MULTIPLE INTELLIGENCES

In 1979, while investigating human potential, world-renowned educator Howard Gardner, PhD, of Harvard University developed his *Theory of Multiple Intelligences.* Gardner's theory states that there are Seven Basic Intelligences, which can combine in any degree of strength within an individual (Celebrating Multiple Intelligences, 1994 & Armstrong, 1994). They are:

- Word Smart (Linguistic Intelligence). This is the capacity to use words effectively, whether oral or written. Reading and writing comes easily to such people.

- Logic Smart (Logical-Mathematical Intelligence). Individuals who possess this kind of intelligence use numbers effectively and reason well. Think of Albert Einstein and Bill Gates.

- Picture Smart (Spatial Intelligence). These people, who are able to perceive the visual-spatial world accurately, tend to think in images and pictures.

- Body Smart (Bodily-Kinesthetic Intelligence). Body Smart people are able to use the entire body as a means of expression, as well as using their hands to produce or alter things.

- Music Smart (Musical Intelligence). The capacity to appreciate, create, critique, and/or express yourself through music is the mark of those who possess this kind of intelligence.

- People Smart (Interpersonal Intelligence). People Smart people know how to "read" other people and interact effectively with them.

- Self Smart (Intrapersonal Intelligence). These very special people have an accurate knowledge of themselves and the ability to adapt based on that knowledge. They enjoy quiet time, writing in journals, and reflecting on experiences.

Dr. Gardner's revolutionary theory has led educators to realize that all students possess, to some degree or another, any or all of these intelligences. The kid in the class you always thought was a "loser" might, in fact, be way ahead in the Picture Smart and Body Smart departments. If you've never thought of yourself as "intelligent," we suggest you take the following exercise to determine what kinds of intelligences you're strong in. (Although our guess is that, based on your choice to be in the beauty and image field, you are high on Picture Smart and Body Smart with, hopefully, a good measure of People Smart thrown in).

GREY MATTER

Now that we've established that intelligence comes in different forms, let's look at where intelligence stems from: the brain.

Make two fists and place them together with your thumbs on top and your arms touching from wrist to elbow. Presto! You've just made a model (a very rough model) of a human brain. The brain, which weighs about three pounds, is the conductor who leads the orchestra known as your body. Each instrument—eyes, mouth, nose, ear, legs, hands, feet, and so on—awaits instruction from the conductor, Maestro Brain. And Maestro Brain does it all: regulates basic life support systems such as breathing; controls all your movements; situates you in your environment so that you recognize things like your house, your car, and your office; and feels, remembers, thinks, reasons, and creates.

Hey, it's a big job but somebody's got to do it, right? The good news is that the brain is up to the task. This amazing organ is made of billions of *neurons*, cells so tiny that 30,000 of them would fit on the head of a pin. Chemicals called *neurotransmitters* pass along from one neuron to another, activating electrical impulses. Each time a particular group of neurons is activated, a certain perception, feeling, thought, or memory is activated. And each time you learn something new—a cooking lesson, let's say, that introduces you to a spice called cumin—your neurons are making all kinds of connections to store away data (the smell, color, and taste of that spice) for future use. Amazing, no?

The human brain's ability to deal with complex perceptions, thoughts, and feelings is the key to our success as a species. Sure, we're not as fast as a cheetah, as strong as an ox, or as eagle-eyed as an eagle, but we can use our brains to make up for our physical limitations. We can create tools—cars, forklifts, binoculars—to accomplish what we need to do. Humans survive because our brains are constantly computing the information that comes in from the environment. Because humans can learn and remember (don't pet the poisonous snake!), we have not only survived but we have thrived.

As powerful as the brain is, however, it has its limitations. It can only really pay attention to one train of conscious thought at a time (except for those rare individuals who can conduct two separate phone conversations simultaneously). The brain also stands to be overtaxed, and so is always trying to get rid of excess information through the process known as forgetting. Too much forgetting, however, can be a dangerous thing, particularly for a student such as yourself, and that brings us to another critical process: remembering.

AH YES, I REMEMBER IT WELL...

Remembering things is right at the top of any brain's job description. Your name, your address, date of birth, the month and year, who the president is, who the president was during the Civil War...little things like that. Without memory, other learning and thinking skills would be impossible. Imagine trying to become a stylist if every day, when you woke up, you were seeing the names Paul Mitchell and Jheri Redding as if for the first time! Your brain stores a vast amount of information in memory, some important (your name), others trivial (the name of the actor who played Mr. Whipple in the Charmin commercials).

How does memory work? Why do we remember certain things and not others? How does the important get lost and the trivial stay lodged in our brain (ever try to get a commercial jingle out of your head while trying to sleep?). With the answers to these questions, we can actually start to improve our ability to remember...and hence become better and better students.

How Does Memory Work?

Memory is usually divided into three stages: (1) **sensory memory**, (2) **short-term memory**, and (3) **long-term memory**. Figure 3-1 is a diagram of the three-stage model of memory.

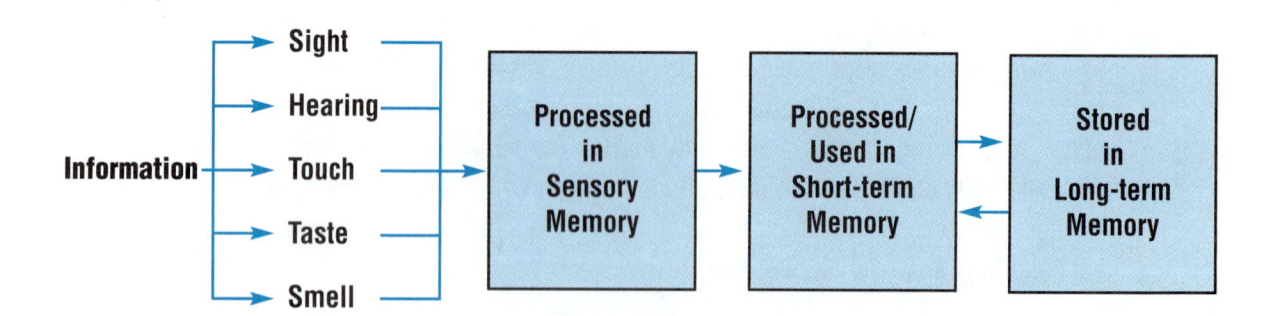

FIGURE 3-1 The three stages of memory are sensory memory, short-term memory, and long-term memory.

Before you can remember anything, you have to *perceive* it through your sight, your hearing, your smell, taste, or any combination thereof. Everything you perceive is registered in *sensory memory*, the first stage of memory. The great French novelist Marcel Proust wrote a massive series of novels entitled *Remembrance of Things Past*, which begins with a character's sensory memory of a madeline (a French, ladyfinger-like cake) he tasted in his youth. The material in sensory memory lasts less than a couple of seconds while your brain processes it, looking to retain what's important, and then most of it is lost.

Some material in sensory memory reaches the second stage, *short-term memory*, where it lasts about twenty seconds. To make it into short-term memory, the new material is matched with information you have already stored, and a meaningful association or pattern is made: Chihuahuas and Taco Bell, for instance. (Advertising relies heavily on short-term memory.)

The material in short-term memory is the information we are currently using. We can make it linger in our mind through the process of repetition, as in reviewing for a test, which we'll discuss soon. Some short-term material may make it into the third stage of *long-term memory*, consisting of memories that have been stored away for future use: the lullaby your grandmother once sang to you; the rustic fishing cabin you went to with an uncle when you were little; the scary time you had when your brother locked you in the attic. The capacity of long-term memory seems limitless. Even people with degenerative brain diseases, like Alzheimer's, who lose all of their short-term memory, may still be able to retrieve a considerable amount from their long-term memory banks, like scraps of old songs or the name of a neighbor from fifty years ago.

Improving Your Memory

There are several techniques that can help to improve both your short-term and long-term memory. You know the basic ones: make notes and keep lists. Invest in post-its and a well-designed organizer. There are, however, some purely mental memory aids that take advantage of how the brain functions. These are repetition, organization, and **mnemonics**.

Repetition. Repetition is an easy, effective way to improve your short-term memory. Going over something again and again in your head—or even better, saying it out loud—will help lodge it in your short-term memory. This is why we ask people to quiz us on things. (The capital of Alabama is Montgomery. The capital of Alaska is Juneau. The capital of Arizona is Phoenix...)

Organization. To help keep something in your short-term memory, try organizing it into seven or fewer chunks. A grocery list of twenty items, for instance, can be "chunked" into produce, dairy, deli, meats, cleaning products, paper goods, and so on.

The best way to organize material for long-term storage is through association between the new material you are trying to memorize and other information you've already stored away. For example, if you're trying to remember to buy some flounder for dinner, you could associate it with the meal you're planning. Chips and...fish! Or you could associate it with a song (if there was a song about a flounder) or with any variety of sounds, images, people, or places.

Another organizing principle for long-term memory has to do with rearranging or categorizing something by meaning, sound, familiarity, alphabetic order, size, or any other pattern that makes sense to you.

Mnemonics. In a variety of situations, we can rely on *mnemonic* devices—little tricks of the mind that help us lodge things in our short-term or even long-term memory. A famous example is the acronym HOMES to remember the five Great Lakes (Huron, Ontario, Michigan, Erie, and Superior). You can make up your own mnemonics whenever you want. Take the shopping expedition for example. You know you have to buy milk, eggs, cheese, ham, and ice cream. Cleverly, you arrange the first letters in each item to make up the word CHIME. Then you walk around the store and it's a piece of cake (no—that was cheese!).

TEN TIPS FOR A HEALTHY BRAIN

You rest your eyes, you soak your feet, you get a backrub, you put moisturizer on your face. So how about a little Tender Loving Care for your brain? Here's how.

1. **Get enough rest.** Most people need at least eight hours. Don't try to exist on half that. It catches up with you and you lose.
2. **Do aerobic exercise.** Jogging, walking, swimming, biking...all improve the flow of blood and oxygen to your brain.
3. **Do mental exercises.** Limber up with puzzles, games—anything to give the ol' brain a good workout.
4. **Eat a balanced, low-fat diet.** Low-fat diets are not only good for your heart but help brain function as well. Just make sure your diet is balanced, with the necessary nutrients for healthy brain function.

> ## TEN TIPS FOR A HEALTHY BRAIN (Continued)
>
> 5. **Eat protein foods.** Foods of animal origins, beans, seeds, and nuts all help to increase alertness and energize your mind. Proteins carry the building blocks of neurotransmitters that increase mental activity.
> 6. **Eat carbohydrate foods.** We're talking about healthy carbs, like whole grains, fruits and vegetables, not Cheese Doodles and Pork Rinds. Carbohydrates help to calm and focus you.
> 7. **Eat fatty fish.** Remember the "myth" that fish was brain food? Well, guess what? It is! Tuna and sardines, among other fish, really do boost your thinking abilities.
> 8. **Don't drink too much caffeine.** It may make you feel more awake for a while, but the brain's no fool, and when it catches on, you'll crash.
> 9. **Don't abuse drugs, including alcohol.** Want a pickled brain? You know where to turn.
> 10. **Wear a helmet when motorcycling, biking, in-line skating.** Now there's a "no-brainer" if ever there was one!
>
> (Sources: Blaun, 1996; Sandmaier, 1996 & Wurtman, 1986).

CRITICAL CONDITION

Whoa! You may think that being in critical condition sounds highly unhealthy, but we only mean it in a positive way. We're talking about getting yourself into the habit of **critical thinking**. When you think critically, you are evaluating what's true and valuable. But to do this, you have to be able to reason well, think logically, and distinguish fact from opinion.

Logic

The word "logic" might bring to mind some kind of philosopher figure, thinking in ways you could never hope to match. But you use logic every day, even if you're not aware of it. When you're hungry, you eat. When you want to find out the time, you look at a clock. If you're cold, you put on a sweater. In all these cases, you've used a logical sequence of steps to get you where you need to be.

One type of logical thinking is called **deductive reasoning**, in which the conclusion that is reached is true because the underlying information on which it is based, called the *premise*, is true. It works like this:

Premise	When it rains, the streets get wet.
Premise	It is raining.
Conclusion	The street is wet.

From this deductive reasoning process, you may jump to yet another deductive reasoning process.

Premise Umbrellas protect against rain.

Premise If I go out in the rain, I will get wet.

Conclusion I will protect myself from the rain with an umbrella.

The conclusion in a deductive reasoning process is always true if the premises are true.

Another type of logical thinking in which the conclusion is not always true is called inductive reasoning. Here, the conclusion drawn is probably true but you have to make sure.

Premise Coworkers Francine and Bill have the same last name.

Premise Francine and Bill leave the office together every day.

Conclusion Francine and Bill are married.

Highly probable, but what if they turn out to be brother and sister? Or just two people named "Smith" who are in a carpool together?

EXERCISE 3-1 Draw Your Own Conclusions

Read each of the following set of premises. If you can reach a logical or probable conclusion, write it down. Say whether you used deductive or inductive reasoning.

1. If a hurricane is predicted, the barrier islands are evacuated.

    A hurricane is predicted.

    Conclusion: _____

    Type of reasoning: _____

2. When I'm in love, I'm happy.

    I'm happy.

    Conclusion: _____

    Type of reasoning: _____

3. Max used his computer to surf the Internet.

    Max used his computer yesterday.

    Conclusion: _____

    Type of reasoning: _____

Fact or Opinion?

It's important to know the difference between a fact and an opinion. If you're watching commercials, listening to politicians, or being dealt a salespitch, it really helps to know that *facts* can be proved to be true while *opinions* are based on values and assumptions that may not be true. A fact is that George Washington was our first president. An opinion is that he was our greatest president.

To distinguish between fact and opinion, you have to be able to think logically. You have to evaluate the available material and sort out that which is true from that which is there to push our emotional buttons. Until you're able to do that, don't go out and buy a used car by yourself.

EXERCISE 3-2 What Do You Think?

Indicate which of the following is fact and which is opinion by writing *fact* or *opinion* in the space provided.

1. Living in the suburbs is better than living in the city.   _____
2. Mixing blue and yellow gives you green.   _____
3. On average, women live longer than men.   _____
4. You should never let your hair go grey before 60.   _____
5. Swimming is good exercise.   _____

CALLING ALL PROBLEM SOLVERS!

When you've developed the ability to solve problems, you'll be very much in demand wherever you go. Both in the office and among family and friends, people who are good at solving problems become natural leaders and are in the position of genuinely helping other people.

To be a good problem-solver, you must be able to think critically. Sometimes, in a crisis, a great deal of hysteria is flying around, and good problem solvers are able to cut through all that with some sound, logical, critical thinking. In addition, however, you have to be sensitive to the fact that problems often carry an emotional component that makes it hard to deal with them in a purely logical way.

Proactive versus Reactive Attitudes

Jan and Lesley have chairs next to each other at Basic Concepts Beauty Salon. Lesley is always taking Jan's things without bothering to put them back.

Jan is going crazy but she says to herself, "Forget about it. Why should I have to deal with this? I'm not the boss. I don't have time to deal with this." With this attitude, is it likely that Jan is going to solve any problems? No way.

Jan's sister Maureen, however, happens to be a good problem solver. When Jan tells Maureen what's been going on, Maureen comes up with a suggestion. Why not go out and buy a few extra combs and such and give them to Lesley, saying you thought she might like these because you've noticed that she's been using yours and you've been looking for them. Jan resists at first, but tries it, and, before long, Lesley has not only stopped "borrowing" but she's giving Jan items that she thinks Jan will appreciate!

The two approaches toward problem-solving that you've just read about can be termed **reactive responses** and **proactive responses**. The reactive approach is an essentially negative one: you react to a problem with a sense of powerlessness and you tend to wind up blaming somebody else for it. On the other hand, a person with a proactive approach takes the matter in hand, deals with it swiftly and effectively, and goes on about her business.

Three Basic Steps Toward Problem-Solving

Clearly, a proactive approach to problem-solving is always the one to go with. Now we have to consider the thought processes involved. Some people rely on trial-and-error, but that's time-consuming and can easily backfire. A better approach is to break problem-solving down into steps. First, *analyze* your problem. Second, go into an *investigative* mode. Third, *decide* on a solution.

Analyzing.
Analyzing a problem means having a good long look at it from all angles so you can then determine what your problem actually is. Amy, for instance, was late for a class one morning and, in the rush, locked her house keys inside. All the windows were locked, so she couldn't climb through a window. Her roommate was not due back until evening. Amy's problem—at least what she thought was her problem—was how to get into the house.

But then Amy stepped back a bit and did some important analyzing. She had her car keys. She didn't need to get into the house until evening. All she needed was to make sure that her roommate, Dana, came home when she said she would. The problem then became redefined through analysis: How will Amy make sure that Dana is home to let in her later?

Investigating.
Some problems take months or years to research, with consulting firms and civil engineers and a corps of experts all hired to help out. Other problems are a snap to investigate, like Amy's. It involved a phone call to Dana's office, whereupon Dana heard the problem and assured Amy she'd be home by seven.

Deciding. Once you've done your analysis and investigating, you can then make a decision as to your best course of action. Dana was coming home by seven, which was a little later than Amy would have wished, but Amy could go to the school library and do some "investigating" for that paper she had to write. In other words, *no problemo!*

EXERCISE 3-3 Solve a Problem

Reneé has a problem. Her boyfriend is violently allergic to her cat. What to do?

1. Analyze the problem and write a one-sentence statement that describes it:
   _____
   _____
   _____

2. Investigate solutions:
   _____
   _____
   _____

3. Decide on the best solution:
   _____
   _____
   _____

LET'S GET CREATIVE

There's thinking and then there's *thinking*. Everyone in the world has to deal with the problem of earwax at some point or another; one person had the idea of putting some cotton on the end of a stick and creating a swab. Many people think of creativity as the exclusive province of artists, writers, directors, and so forth, rather than ordinary people. But while it's true that some people dedicate themselves to creativity, all people have the potential to think creatively and to use that creative thinking in their own pursuits.

Psychologists define creativity as the ability to see things in a new way and to come up with unusual and effective solutions to problems. Creativity can rest as much with an assistant as it can with a boss. In fact, that's how some assistants become boss!

What makes for creativity? Intelligence, you may be surprised to learn, bears little relation to creativity. Many highly intelligent people are not creative thinkers. Rather, creative people tend to be those who are intrinsically motivated (motivation that comes from within). They choose to do what they do because they love doing it. Creative people perform tasks without fear of being judged foolish. They are not afraid to make mistakes.

Upping Your C.Q. (Creative Quotient)

Creativity depends not so much on talent or intelligence as on how we use our brains. Most of us use our brains in solid, predictable ways, but creative thinkers achieve their breakthroughs by tapping into other modes of thinking. The techniques described here all focus on getting us to change our routine thought processes.

Associative Thinking. If you're looking to get a real jump start on your creative thinking, try thinking associatively. This is a method in which you let your mind wander from one thing to another, sometimes seemingly even unrelated, in order to gain some fresh insight on a problem.

Back-burner Thinking. Sometimes when you spend too much time thinking about a problem, you burn out and nothing is accomplished. This is the time to put the problem on the "back burner." Back-burner thinking involves knowing when to stop consciously thinking about a problem so your unconscious can come riding in for the rescue.

Mind-mapping. Mind-mapping is related to associative thinking. It is a creative technique that draws on visual, intuitive thought processes that we often neglect when we're trying to solve a problem. In mind-mapping, you sketch out your problem or topic and the thoughts that come to mind. The result is a drawing—a visual representation of your ideas. When drawing a mind-map, follow these steps:

- Draw a picture of the problem or issue in the center of a piece of paper.
- Print key words and ideas, and connect these to the central drawing.
- Use colors, images, symbols, and codes to emphasize important points.
- Use associative thinking to come up with more ideas, and connect them with other parts of the mind map.

When you've done the above, look at your mind-map and see if any new patterns have emerged that can help you with your problem.

Brainstorming. Many work environments factor in **brainstorming** as a crucial part of the job. Brainstorming allows a group of people—from five to eight is best—to come up with as many ideas about a problem or issue as they

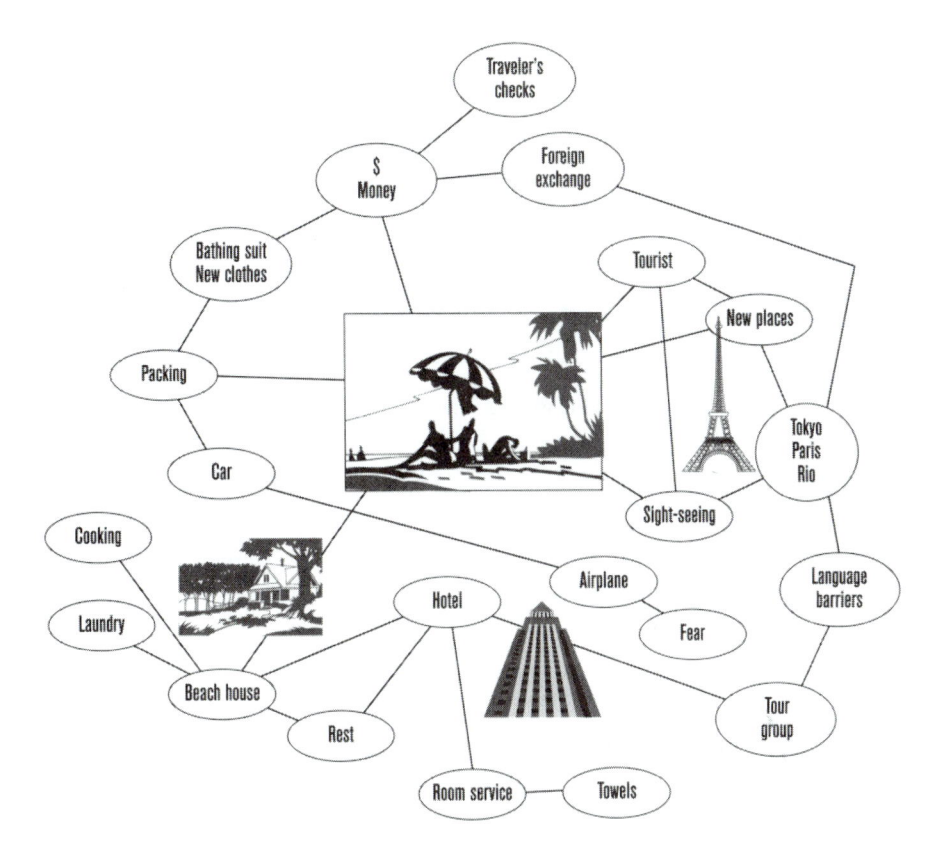

FIGURE 3-2 In mind-mapping, you sketch the topic and ideas that come to mind.

can. To brainstorm effectively, people have to learn certain rules, like not coming down critically on other people and listening when other people are talking. At first, it can feel competitive and pressured, but, when you get used to it, it can provide an exciting intellectual ride you'll want to repeat again and again.

EXERCISE 3-5 Brainstorm Ahead!

With five or more people from your class, stage a brainstorming session on this topic: Finding a job in the beauty and image field.

One person should take notes on the ideas that come up. When the session is done, answer the following questions.

1. What did the group decide was important to do when looking for a job in the field?

_____
_____

2. Did everyone contribute an idea? If not, why not?
   _____
   _____

3. Were any of the ideas you contributed inspired by something someone else said?
   _____
   _____

4. Do you think you would have come up with these ideas on your own? Explain.
   _____
   _____

TIME TO STUDY

No matter how good you are at critical thinking and problem-solving, your life as a student is going to be difficult until you get some really good study habits under your belt. You'll need a good place to study, a schedule to stick to, and clear learning goals.

Setting Up a Study Area

Some people study best in an atmosphere of absolute silence, like a library carrel. Others do better with a little outside stimulation, whether it's a reading room, a lounge, or the kitchen table. No matter how you like it, the point is to have some consistency in where you study.

Your dream study area might have a lounger, a stereo system, a half-refrigerator stocked with Rocky Road ice cream and so on, but that's not really necessary. Focus instead on the essentials, which you can figure out by asking yourself a few key questions:

- Where should the study area be located?
- What kind of furniture, if any, will you need?
- How will you decorate the area to make it functional, pleasant, and inspiring? What light, color, sound, pictures, and objects will you use?
- What equipment and supplies will you need? Will you need a computer or can you get by with the computer lab?
- What other resources do you need to invest in, such as dictionaries, calculators, electric pencil sharpener, and so on?

Once you set up your area, be on guard for typical problems, which can include:

- Too much noise (If you can't get around this, try earplugs).
- Too little noise (Some people go batty in utter silence. Use a portable tape deck or boom box with headphones for that added stimulation you need).
- Visual distractions (Maybe you can screen off your study area?).
- Interruptions (Ask people to not disturb you during certain "sacred" study hours. Use a phone answering machine if necessary).
- Discomfort (You may have to invest in a good chair or other aids).

Stay on Schedule

Once you've got your place under control, you really have to establish a consistent schedule for yourself. Studying is not something you should be trying to fit in between racquetball, *Baywatch* and a jaunt to the nearest donut shop.

If you think your schedule is too overloaded to allow for daily studying, review your day and see where you can steal some time. How about on your commute? If you're on a bus or a train, why not? Perhaps you have time after work or after dinner. Also, be aware of your body clock and when it is easiest for you to study. Some people do best first thing in the morning; others are night owls who can't really get going until after the rest of us are asleep.

EXERCISE 3-5 Early Bird or Night Owl?

For each of the following statements, answer *true* or *false* to get a better sense of your peak studying time.

1. I would wake up early even if my alarm didn't go off. _____
2. When I have something to do that requires concentration, I do it first thing in the morning. _____
3. If I stay up late to get something done, I often fall asleep over it. _____
4. It usually takes me all morning to get started. _____
5. I would rather go to school or work in the afternoon instead of the morning. _____
6. When I have to concentrate on something, it's best if I work on it after lunch. _____

7. I could stay up all night. _____
8. I usually start tasks that require concentration after dinner. _____
9. I wish I could relax during the day and go to work or school at night. _____

Here's how to figure out your peak learning time:

If you answered true to items 1-3, your best time is the morning.

If you answered true to items 4-6, your best time is the afternoon.

If you answered true to items 7-9, your best time is the evening.

Set Study Goals for Yourself

Do you remember our discussion of short-term goals? Studying is a perfect example of a short-term goal. If you study for a test, you can usually achieve a good grade on it. Simple as that. Focusing on a short-term goal like studying helps you progress toward your intermediate- and long-term goals.

STUDY TIPS

You've got a lot of reading to do now. So let us clue you in to a helpful method called the *P.Q.R. system*.

Previewing

Previewing means scanning an assigned reading selection to look for the main points and to discover how the material is organized. It's like a mini-orientation that sets you up for where you want to go. If you're previewing a book, you could skim the preface and the table of contents. When previewing a chapter, look through it for subheadings. To preview an article, scan any headings and check out graphs, charts, or other illustrations.

Questioning

Once you start reading, make yourself into an active reader by questioning the material. Ask yourself, Why am I reading this? How will it serve me? As you continue to read, use the words *who, what, where, when, why,* and *how* to fix you in place as you go along. This technique helps you to master the material and commit it to your long-term memory.

Reviewing

Reading something once when you study doesn't do the trick. To fix it in your long-term memory, you have to review, most effectively by using three processes: seeing, saying, and writing.

Go back over the material, *see* it, *say* the main points out loud, and then *write* out brief study notes that outline the main ideas.

TAKING NOTES

Notetaking is another important skill to master as you become a more serious student. You should use a spiral notebook or looseleaf binder with ruled paper for your notes. Set up sections or separate notebooks for each course. There are several techniques that will help you get the most out of notetaking. They are formatting your notes, outlining, and diagramming.

Using a Two-Column Format

Many students find that a two-column format (Figure 3-3), with one narrow and one wide column, works best for notetaking. The narrow column is used for *recall words*, important words that provide cues for the main ideas. These are filled in when you review your notes, not when you first take them. The wide column is used for main ideas and important facts.

Outlining and Documenting

When you take notes, you're not trying to capture every word your instructor speaks. You're going for the main ideas and important facts. To save time, use phrases and abbreviations rather than full sentences. The outline form, if only with indentations rather than actual numbers, allows you to visually grasp the relationship of main ideas to secondary ideas or supporting details. Other devices that may be helpful include:

- Time lines—good for showing the sequence of historical events.
- Flow charts—can be used to show the steps in a process or procedure.
- Pie charts—show the relationship of parts to a whole.
- An idea diagram—like a mind map, it shows the relationship of secondary ideas to a main idea and to one another.
- Drawing—gives an instant description of something visual.

	Evaluating Software Oct. 10
Hardware requirements	Check that computer system matches hardware requirements:
	• IBM-compatible or Macintosh
	• type of processor needed
	• which operating system? (Windows 3.1 or 95)
	• amount of memory needed to run the program (RAM)
	• amount of free space on hard drive
	• monitor type
	• 3.5" disks or CD-ROM or Internet download
Documentation	"How to" manual (documentation) and/or help system
	• complete
	• well-organized
	• easy to find what you need (good index)
	• tech. support available
Installation	Installation
	• clear instructions
	• fast & easy
	Easy to learn
	Does what it's supposed to
	Cost

FIGURE 3-3 The two-column format is a popular note-taking technique for students.

USING THE LIBRARY

Your school's library should be viewed as an essential resource for your education. Expect to spend a lot of time there or at your local public library and get to know them well. Enroll in an orientation course. All libraries offer them and librarians are more than happy to teach basic library skills. They will show you how to use the card catalog, research periodicals and reference works, and even how to use the Internet if you are not yet familiar with it.

TAKING TESTS

After studying comes test-taking and this is butterflies-in-the-stomach time for a lot of us. This can be alleviated, however, by good preparation. Banish from your life the "all-nighter" and substitute the much more effective regimen of studying in short sessions of no more than two hours. And remember: studying for a test means reviewing what you have already learned, not learning it from scratch! That means going to your notes, giving careful review to your narrow column of "recall words," and coming up with a variety of memory devices we described above, like associative thinking, mnemonics, and "chunking" to help things sink into your brain.

Preparing for a Test

If you're an anxious test-taker, prepare not with coffee or cola but, instead, have a calming carbohydrate snack (not junk food, but grains, fruits, or vegetables) and try to make sure you've had a good night's sleep. A little Mozart works wonders, too. Be prepared by having all your necessary test materials—pens, pencils, calculator, watch, books, and so on—assembled the night before, so there's one less thing to think about on test day.

Basic Test-Taking Techniques

There are some basic approaches to test-taking you should know about. Here are some suggestions:

- **Skim the whole test first.** This preview, or overview, orients you to the test and clues you in to the most important parts of it.

- **Pace yourself.** Know how much each question is worth and budget your time accordingly. Check your watch or clock as you proceed.

- **Answer the easy questions first.** Don't get hung up on the hard ones. Put a check in the margin next to those and come back to them.

- **Make sure you understand each question.** Underline key words and ideas. If you think a question is vague or unclear, ask your instructor for help. Test-creators can do just as poorly as test-takers.

- **Looks for clues to the answer in the question itself.** For example, when answering true-false questions, look for the words *always* or *never*. These words often signal a false statement.

Welcome to the World

You're now more in charge of your life than you've ever been, and that includes your education. Your parents and your teachers are not going to be riding herd on you as they once did, and, with the cost of tuition, the stakes are higher than ever. The good news, however, is that the sense of personal satisfaction promises to be higher than ever too. You're calling the shots and chances are you'll discover that learning is one of life's most exciting experiences. And it's an exciting experience that never has to end!

REFERENCES

Armstrong, T. (1994). *Multiple intelligences in the classroom.* Association for Supervision and Curriculum Development.

Blaun, R. (1996, May/June). How to eat smart. *Psychology Today*, 35.

Celebrating multiple intelligences: Teaching for success. (1994). The New City School.

Sandmaier, M. (1996, March). Eat your way to a good mood. *Good Housekeeping*, 93-94.

Wurtman, J. J. (1986). *Managing your mind and mood through food* (pp. 18-23). New York: Rawson Associates.

ROUTE FOUR

THE WHOLE YOU: HEAD TO TOE

KEY TERMS

holistic
anorexia nervosa
bulimia
circadian rhythm

In your readings, you may have come across the word "holistic," as in holistic medicine, but perhaps you have only a vague sense of what it means. The word **holistic** means "to emphasize the organic or functional relation between the parts and the whole of something" and the term *holistic approach* means "to emphasize the person as a whole, not as a set of isolated functions or disorders."

Why do we mention the term "holistic"? Because even though we are reaching you as a student, at your school, we are addressing the "whole" of who you are; we are also advocating that *you* look at life with a holistic eye. After all, you play many parts in life— you are someone's child or perhaps someone's parent or someone's partner; you are a student; you may be an employee; you may be a member of an athletic team or a musical organization or a drama group; and there are probably many other facets that make up who you are today. That's why we're interested in looking at the *whole* of you—hence, the holistic approach.

One aspect of "the whole you" that demands special attention is your physical condition. In this day and age of health awareness, it is generally understood that a strong and healthy body provides the foundation for all your activities and profoundly influences your state of mind. A feeling of physical well-being is vital in helping you to realize your potential in all areas of your life.

YOU ARE WHAT YOU EAT

So goes the famous old saying. Perhaps one reason why this saying has been around so long is because there's a great deal of truth to it. What you put into your body has tremendous bearing on how you function; studies show that most Americans aren't very informed or disciplined about what they put into their bodies. That, combined with insufficient exercise, inadequate rest, and widespread abuse of alcohol and tobacco, can wreak havoc on ambitions and the ability to realize one's potential.

On the other hand, people who take good care of their bodies are rewarded by increased well-being and self-confidence (not to mention a possible upswing in their social lives!). The first step in taking good care of your body has to do with feeding your body. It is important to familiarize yourself with the major nutrients and know how they affect your health. You should also know how to classify foods into the basic five food groups and how to use a Food Guide Pyramid to select your foods.

Nutrients

Let's have a quick orientation session about *nutrients*, the substances that your body uses for growth, maintenance, and repair, as well as for energy. It's important to have an overview of this subject so that you can guard yourself from becoming susceptible to the latest fad diet (see Table 4-1). Such diets often rule out some central food group and can cause serious damage to your health.

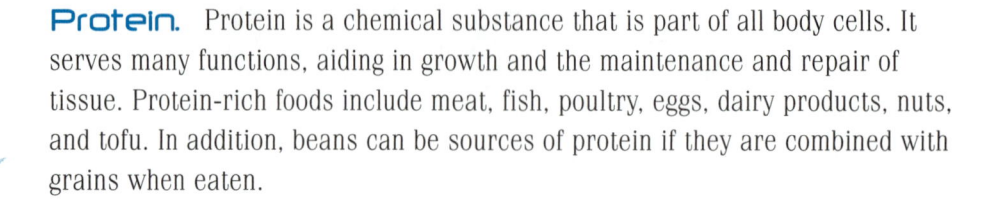

Protein. Protein is a chemical substance that is part of all body cells. It serves many functions, aiding in growth and the maintenance and repair of tissue. Protein-rich foods include meat, fish, poultry, eggs, dairy products, nuts, and tofu. In addition, beans can be sources of protein if they are combined with grains when eaten.

TABLE 4-1 Nutrients and Their Sources

NUTRIENTS	MAJOR FUNCTIONS	MAJOR SOURCES
Protein	Growth, maintenance of tissue, enzymes and hormones to regulate body processes	Meat, fish, poultry, beans, eggs, nuts, dairy products, tofu
Carbohydrates	Primary sources of energy; fiber aids digestion	Bread, cereal, rice, pasta, and other grain products: fruits, vegetables, potatoes; sweets
Fats	Concentrated storage of energy; insulation, dissolves certain vitamins	Meats, fish, poultry, and dairy products; ails, lard, margarine; fried foods
Water	Present in all cells. Transports nutrients and wastes, takes part in many chemical reactions, cushions, regulates body temperature	All beverages. Also present to a degree in all foods
Vitamin A	Growth, healthy skin, bones and teeth, good vision	Meat, egg yolk, dairy products, dark green leafy and deep-yellow vegetables
Thiamin (Vitamin B_1)	Helps use carbohydrates for energy, maintains healthy nervous system	Whole-grain products, enriched breads and cereals, meat, poultry, fish, beans, nuts, egg yolk
Riboflavin (Vitamin B_2)	Contributes to use of proteins, carbohydrates, and fats for energy; healthy skin	Dairy products, organ meat, green leafy vegetables, enriched breads and cereals
Niacin (Vitamin B_3)	Healthy nervous system, skin, digestion	Poultry, meat, fish, beans, nuts, dark green leafy vegetables, potatoes, whole-grain or enriched breads and cereals
Ascorbic acid (Vitamin C)	Helps build material that holds cells together, healthy teeth, gums, and blood vessels, helps body resist infection and heal wounds	Citrus fruits and their juices, tomatoes, broccoli, raw green vegetables
Vitamin D	Needed to absorb calcium and phosphorus, healthy bones and teeth	Milk, egg yolk, liver, herring, sardines, tuna, salmon (body can make this vitamin with direct sunlight on the skin)
Vitamin E	Protects cells from oxidation (antioxidant)	Vegetable oils, margarine, wheat germ, nuts
Calcium	Needed for structure of healthy bones and teeth, healthy muscles and nerves	Dairy products, broccoli, turnips, collards, kale, mustard greens, oysters, shrimp, salmon, clams
Iodide	Prevents goiter, needed to manufacture enzyme thyroxine	Iodized salt, small amounts in seafood
Iron	Needed for healthy blood and formation of many enzymes	Liver, meat, poultry, shellfish, egg yolk, green leafy vegetables, nuts, enriched cereals and breads
Potassium	Helps in synthesis of protein, fluid balance, healthy nerves and muscles	Citrus fruits, bananas, apricots, meat, fish, and cereal
Sodium (salt)	Helps maintain fluid balance, helps absorption of other nutrients	Table salt; processed food, especially ham, cold cuts, bacon; and salty snacks

Source: Adapted from U.S Department of Agriculture, *Family Fare, A Guide to Good Nutrition*, Home and Garden Bulletin No. 1, 1 97B, and other USDA publications.

Carbohydrates. These substances provide energy for the body, especially the brain and the nervous system. Whole-grain carbohydrates also contain much-needed fiber to aid the digestive system. Flour, cereal, bread, rice, pasta, and other grain products are all good sources of carbohydrates. In addition, some fruits and vegetables as well as all sweets contain carbohydrates.

Fats. In some quarters, fat has become a dirty word, but healthy fats provide concentrated storage of energy for the body. They also provide insulation and dissolve certain vitamins. There are two main types of fat:

1. *Saturated fats* are those that are solid at room temperature, including lard, butter, palm and coconut oils (the latter two are often found in unhealthy baked goods). Saturated fats increase the body's own production of cholesterol, which can be problematic for many individuals.

2. *Unsaturated fats* are liquid at room temperature. Polyunsaturated fats are found in corn, safflower and soybean oil. Monounsaturated fats are found in peanut and olive oils.

Fats and cholesterol, a fatty acid found in meat, cheese, shellfish, and eggs, have been the focus of much attention in recent years and are linked to increased risk of heart disease, stroke, certain cancers, and obesity. Generally, it is wise to cut back on your fat and cholesterol intake. In other words, don't double your fast food order (you might even think about passing up that fat-laden fast food altogether!).

One type of fat that most Americans don't get enough of is Omega-3, a fatty acid needed for proper brain functioning. It is found in tuna, salmon, trout, and sardines.

Water. Good health depends on proper hydration, which means drinking often. Water is better for you than soft drinks, coffee, tea, or just about anything else you can name. It's calorie-free, thirst-quenching and it helps to cushion and lubricate parts of the body, as well as regulate the body's temperature. Drink often...drink deep.

Vitamins and Minerals. In addition to proteins, fats, carbohydrates, and water, foods also contain trace amounts of vitamins and minerals essential for life and growth. Each vitamin and mineral has specific functions in the body. For instance, Vitamin D is needed for healthy bones and teeth while Vitamin A prevents eye problems and boosts immunity. Your diet may be fortified with vitamin and mineral supplements taken as tablets, capsules, and powders (as in shakes). Be sure you do some research, if only in talking to a pharmacist, in selecting brands that are reliable. Vitamin and mineral contents of foods, along with other nutrients, can be determined by reading the *Nutrition Facts* required by law on food packaging. See Table 4-2, which shows you how these facts are typically presented.

TABLE 4-2
Nutrition Facts Chart

Nutrition Facts

Serving Size	1 Pastry (52g)
Servings per Package	8

Amount/Serving

Calories 200 • Fat Calories 50

	% Daily Value*
Total Fat 5g	8%
Saturated Fat 1.0g	5%
Cholesterol 0mg	0%
Sodium 190mg	80/0
Total Carbohydrate 37g	12%
Dietary Fiber 1 g	4%
Sugars 16g	
Protein 2g	

Vitamin A 10% • Vitamin C 0% • Calcium 0%
Iron 10% • Thiamin 10% • Riboflavin 10%
Niacin 10% • Vitamin B_6 10% • Folate 10%
Phosphorus 2%

*Percent Daily Values are based on a 2,000 calorie diet. Your daily values may be higher or lower depending on your calorie needs.

	Calories	2,000	2,500
Total Fat	Less than	65g	80g
Sat. Fat	Less than	20g	25g
Cholesterol	Less than	300mg	300mg
Sodium	Less than	2,400mg	2,400mg
Total Carbohydrate		300g	375g
Dietary Fiber		25g	30g

EXERCISE 4-1 Look at What You're Eating!

Use the Food Diary on the following page to keep track of what you eat or drink for three days. Be honest! Then review your diet. Use the information in Table 4-1 and the nutrition facts in Table 4-2 to determine content of the foods you've eaten to answer the following questions:

1. What foods were your major sources of protein?

   _____

   _____

2. What foods were your major sources of carbohydrates?

   _____

   _____

THREE-DAY FOOD DIARY

Meal	Day 1	Day 2	Day 3
Breakfast			
Lunch			
Dinner			
Snacks			
Beverages			

3. What foods were your major sources of fat?

   _____
   _____

4. During the three days, did you eat food that provides all the vitamins and minerals listed in the Table?

   _____

   If not, what vitamins and minerals did you miss?

   _____
   _____

   What should you eat to make sure you get the missing vitamin(s) and mineral(s)?

   _____
   _____
   _____
   _____
   _____
   _____

WHAT IS A BALANCED DIET?

Years ago, the typical business lunch was a porterhouse steak, a baked potato with butter and sour cream, a Caesar salad, a slice of New York cheesecake, and two or three martinis to wash it all down. Today, it's a chef's salad and Perrier. Ah, times have changed.

The U.S. Department of Agriculture (USDA) and the U.S. Department of Health and Human Services issue Dietary Guidelines for Americans. Their basic advice is to:

- Eat a variety of foods.
- Maintain a healthy body weight.
- Eat foods that are low in fat, saturated fat, and cholesterol.
- Eat plenty of vegetables, fruits, and grain products.
- Limit sugars (including granulated sugar, syrups, jellies, honey, candy, and soft drinks).
- Limit salt (including such high-sodium foods as canned soups and luncheon meats).
- Avoid or limit alcohol.

To ensure that you get a healthy variety of food, it's helpful to structure your diet around the five food groups. Another way to make sure you get what you need is to use the Food Guide Pyramid.

Five Food Groups

During the Reagan administration, when budget cuts were happening in all the social programs, some great minds decided that catsup should be considered a "vegetable" serving in school lunches and would thus qualify as a daily serving under the Five Food Groups rule. That was a really bad idea. A really good idea, however, is for you to know what the Five Food Groups are and to try to live your life accordingly. The basic five food groups include:

1. **Grains**. Whole-grain breads, cereals, tortillas, brown rice, and pasta are the healthiest of the grain products. Other grain products include white rice, muffins, waffles, sweetened cereals, doughnuts, pastry, and stuffing. Some of these contain high levels of sugar, salt, or fats that make them a no-no under certain conditions.

2. **Vegetables**. Most vegetables are extremely beneficial and you can eat as much of them as you care to. There are some exceptions, of course. Canned vegetables, french fries, and pickles all contain added sugars, salt, or fats that make them less than healthy choices.

3. **Fruits**. Fresh fruits are good for you, but canned fruits often contain added sugar. (Many canned fruits, however, are available in unsweetened form). Dried fruit also packs a lot of calories.

4. **Dairy products**. Skim and 1 percent milk products and nonfat yogurt have the least fat of any dairy products. Ice milk, frozen low-fat yogurt, and 2 percent milk have moderate amounts of fat. Highest in fat are whole milk, cream and sour cream, cheeses, and ice cream.

5. **Meat, poultry, fish, eggs, beans, and nuts**. In this group, the choices with the least fat and salt are most fish, poultry without the skin, lean cuts of beef and pork, egg whites, and beans, peas, and lentils. Oil-packed tuna, poultry with skin, most red meat, tofu, peanut butter, nuts, processed meats (cold cuts and hot dogs), and whole eggs have greater amounts of fat.

The Food Guide Pyramid

The Food Guide Pyramid offers a quick, easy, visual representation of how many servings a day you should be eating of each food group. At the base of the pyramid are foods that can be eaten in quantity; at the top are those foods that should be eaten sparingly (Figure 4-1).

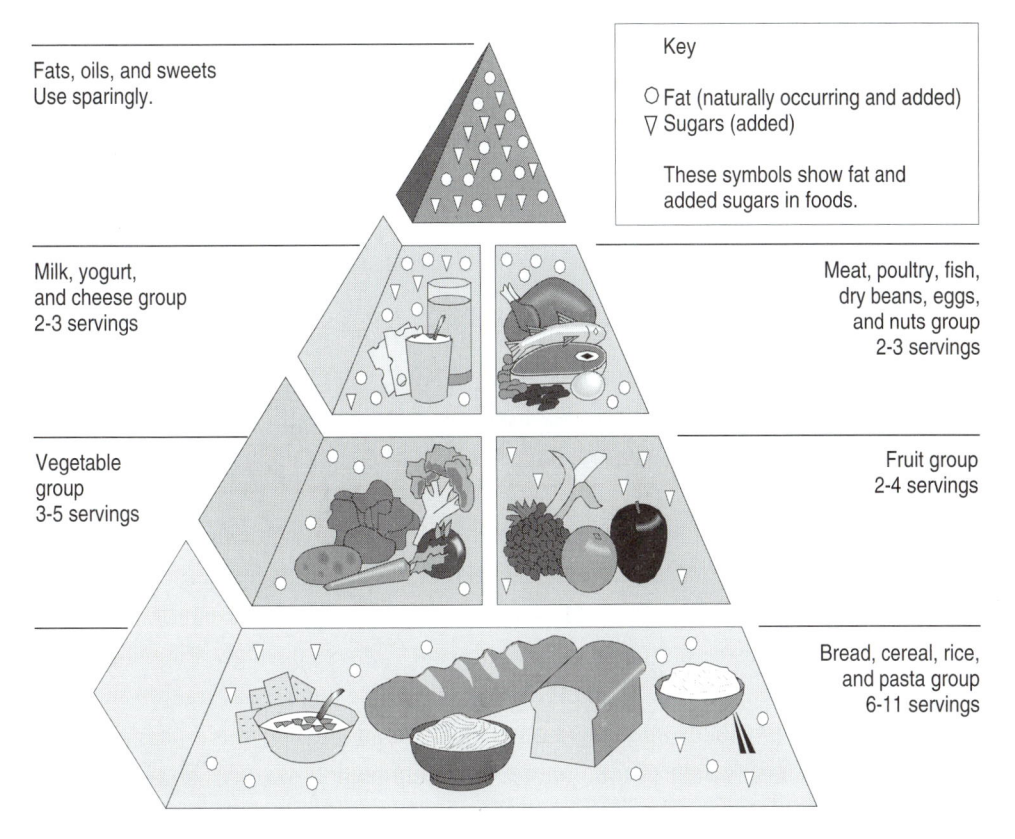

FIGURE 4-1 The Food Guide Pyramid

The number of servings recommended by the USDA varies depending on your age, sex, size, and level of activity:

- Inactive women and some older adults require the fewest servings per day of each group, about 1,600 calories total.

- Children, teenage girls, active women, and inactive men require an average number of servings per day from each group, about 2,200 calories total.

- Teenage boys, active men, and some very active women need the maximum number of servings per day, about 2,800 total.

If you visualize the Food Guide Pyramid as you plan your meals, you'll be able to achieve a balanced diet with variety and moderation.

Getting a Grip

Okay, you're feeling bloated, listless, and you don't like what you're seeing in the mirror. What do you do about it?

The first thing *not* to do is go on some kind of fad diet where you're eating nothing but cantaloupe and buffalo meat for three weeks. Not only can such diets be highly injurious to your health (not to mention the health of the buffalo), but almost inevitably after such a diet you'll gain back not only the weight you've lost but an additional few pounds. This is called "see-saw dieting" and it's the kind of trap that causes you great grief while it fuels a multi-billion dollar American diet industry.

Don't despair, however. If your diet is less than satisfactory, you can change it. The first step is to keep a food diary of what you eat for a few days, as you are doing (or did) in the Three-day Food Diary on page 60. Once you've done that, you can analyze your eating habits and see where they need to be changed.

The next step is to look at the quantity of foods you eat. One out of four Americans are obese as compared to one of out ten French. The reason for this, experts say, has everything to do with the amounts of food eaten. The French will eat cheeses and pastries and oils, but always sparingly. Their breakfasts are small; their dinners are small. We, on the other hand, eat large breakfasts with eggs and pancakes and bacon and sausage and maybe even a piece of pie thrown in. Fast-food lunches and dinners, naturally high in fat, are "doubled." Portions at chain restaurants are absurdly large. That's why there is such a weight problem in this country.

The next consideration is your eating habits. For example, do you skip breakfast? That's a bad habit, because breakfast fuels the start of your day and helps spread your eating into smaller meals. Studies have shown that several small meals each day rather than one or two large meals helps prevent the storage of fat.

If you're a snacker, look at what you're eating. Substitute some fruit for that candy bar. And if you're always eating on the run, prepare ahead. Pack a healthy lunch instead of grabbing a hot dog. It's a little more work, but a lot better for you.

There's a Lot of Help Out There

If maintaining a proper weight (see Table 4-3) is an ongoing problem for you, you can seek help from a variety of sources. Start with your physician, who may refer you to a nutritionist. Keep in mind too that in addition to eating problems, there are also *eating disorders*, which can have grave implications to your health. One such disorder, **anorexia nervosa**, manifests itself when a person loses weight until he or she is 15 percent or more below the ideal weight. In spite of being thin, people who suffer from anorexia nervosa think they are fat and continue to eat very little. The ailment can become so severe that those who suffer from it may refuse to even lick a postage stamp because the glue might

TABLE 4-3 **Suggested Weights for Adults**

	WEIGHT IN POUNDS*	
Height	**19 to 34 Years**	**35 Years and Over**
5'0"	97-128	108-138
5'1"	101-132	111-143
5'2"	104-137	115-148
5'3"	107-141	119-152
5'4"	111-146	122-157
5'5"	114-150	126-162
5'6"	118-155	130-167
5'7"	121-160	134-172
5'8"	125-164	138-178
5'9"	129-169	142-183
5'10"	132-174	146-188
5'11"	136-179	151-194
6'0"	140-184	155-199
6'1"	144-189	159-205
6'2"	148-195	164-210
6'3"	152-200	168-216
6'4"	156-205	173-222
6'5"	160-211	177-228
6'6"	164-216	182-234

*The higher weights in the ranges generally apply to men, who tend to have more muscle and bone: the lower weights apply to women, who have less muscle and bone.

Sources: U.S. Department of Agriculture and U,S. Department of Health and Human Services, *Dietary Guidelines for Americans*. 3rd ed, Washington DC: 1990. p. 9; Data from *Diet and Health: Implications for Reducing Chronic Disease Risk*, National Research Council, Washington DC: National Academy of Sciences, 1989.

---

have a fraction of a calorie. Between 5 and 10 percent of individuals with anorexia nervosa die of starvation or complications of severe weight loss. Singer Karen Carpenter of The Carpenters was perhaps the most famous victim of this disorder.

Bulimia is another eating disorder in which the person secretly binges, eating huge amounts of high-calorie foods, and then purges, either by vomiting or by using laxatives. People with bulimia may or may not be underweight. Because they binge and purge in private, their condition is easy to conceal. The late Princess Diana was a bulimiac who went public with her problem.

Both anorexia nervosa and bulimia are disorders that primarily afflict adolescent girls and young women. The affluent, weight-conscious cultures of the United States and Europe foster a climate in which these girls and young women must measure themselves against an unreal ideal of female beauty typified by rail-thin high fashion models, like Kate Moss. Striving for that look can lead many to crash diets which can, in turn, lead into full-blown eating disorders.

It is important to realize that people who have eating disorders cannot consciously regulate their eating habits. They need the kind of professional help offered by psychotherapists, who may use drugs as part of their treatment.

GETTING FIT

Ringing that "holistic" bell again, we want to remind you that nutrition is only part of the "whole you." Even when you get your eating habits in hand, you're going to want to start paying closer attention to your level of physical activity and how you can fit exercise time into your life (assuming that you can get over the fact that you hate to exercise!).

It's no secret any more that exercise is a very important component of how you live your life. Modern life, with its cars, computers, and TV, has a way of making "couch potatoes" out of the best of us. Most people today do not work in jobs where physical activity is a large part of their ordinary routine. To be active, we must make a conscious decision to exercise or play sports.

But what if you hate to exercise? Hey, *lots* of people hate to exercise, but they do it anyway. Because they know it's good for them. Because it keeps their hearts and lungs and colons and brains in good working order. Because it makes them look good. Do you need more reasons?

EXERCISE 4-2 Rate Your Level of Activity

You can check your level of physical activity by rating how hard, how long, and how often you exercise. Circle your score for each question.

1. How hard do you exercise in a typical session?

	Score
No change in pulse	0
Little change in heart rate (slow walking, bowling, yoga)	1
Small increase in heart rate and breathing (table tennis, active golf)	2
Moderate increase in heart rate and breathing (rapid walking, dancing, easy swimming)	3
Occasional heavy breathing and sweating (tennis, basketball, squash)	4
Sustained heavy breathing and sweating (jogging, aerobic dance)	5

2. How long do you exercise at one session?

Less than 5 minutes	0
5 to 14 minutes	1
15 to 29 minutes	2
30 to 44 minutes	3
45 to 59 minutes	4
60 minutes or more	5

3. How often do you exercise?

Less than once a week	0
Once a week	1
2 times a week	2
3 times a week	3
4 times a week	4
5 times a week	5

4. Now take your scores from each question and multiply them:

_____ x _____ x _____ = Activity level

Rate your activity level as follows:

Score	Activity Level
Less than 15	Inactive
15-24	Somewhat active
25-40	Moderately active
41-60	Active
Over 60	Very active

If your score is 41 or higher, you are active enough to enjoy a wide variety of physical activities. If your score is less than 41, you should approach a change in your physical fitness program gradually and with caution. Anyone who is starting a new or increased fitness program should check with his or her doctor first.

Jump In—The Water's Swell!

The President's Council on Physical Fitness and Sports defines *physical fitness* as the ability to carry out daily tasks without tiring and with enough energy left to enjoy leisure activities and to handle an emergency requiring physical exertion.

Your own level of physical fitness is determined to a large extent by your daily routine. If you spend all day sitting at a computer terminal, you're not getting a lot of physical activity. If, on the other hand, you're a messenger riding around town on a bike, you don't exactly have to worry about fitting time in at the gym.

Most of us these days find ourselves in the first category, and that means to improve our normal level of fitness, we have to add in some exercise, sports, or dance to our regular routine.

There are different aspects to physical fitness, all of which have to be paid attention to and all of which, health permitting, we should be working toward improvement. They are:

- **Cardiorespiratory endurance**. This is the ability to do moderately strenuous activity over a period of time without overtaxing the heart and the lungs.
- **Muscular strength**. This is the ability to exert force in a single try.
- **Muscular endurance**. By this we mean the ability to repeat movements or to hold a position for a long time without tiring.
- **Flexibility**. This is the ability to move a joint through its full range of motion.
- **Body composition**. This has to do with the proportion of muscle compared to fat.

Different physical activities promote the different aspects discussed above. In general, aerobic activities—running, power walking, swimming, basketball, step training, and tennis—are best for developing cardiorespiratory endurance and improved body composition. Activities such as calisthenics, weight training, karate, and yoga improve strength, endurance, and flexibility.

Consider the following aerobic exercises as an activity you might enjoy.

- Aerobic dance is twenty or more minutes of running, skipping, hopping, jumping, sliding, stretching, and bending set to music.
- Step training involves stepping on and off a low bench while doing arm movements. It's a low-impact aerobic activity that offers the same benefits as jogging with fewer risks of injury.
- Walking at a brisk pace is an excellent aerobic activity that requires no special equipment or skill and can be done almost anywhere.
- Jogging is a very popular aerobic exercise that only requires a pair of good jogging sneakers. Joggers sometimes develop leg problems because jogging is a high-impact activity.
- Swimming is often considered the best aerobic activity because water cushions impact as it exercises all the major muscle groups.
- Bicycling, whether stationary or on the road, has aerobic benefits when it is done briskly for long distances.
- Cross-country skiing (simulated on a Nordic track machine) provides excellent aerobic benefits.

Sticking to the Plan

Many people start an exercise program with the very best of intentions but after a few months, those intentions, and their resolve, fall by the wayside. To avoid that happening, and to ensure that physical activity remains a real part of your routine, consider the following guidelines:

1. Choose a friend or relative you can rely on and make an agreement with them to exercise. Be sure to write it down.

2. Be specific. Write down the days you will exercise, what you will be doing, and the number of months you will do it.

3. Include rewards and punishments. Specify what you'll do to earn a reward (a chocolate-dipped strawberry perhaps?) and what punishment you will dole out when you skip a session (watching *Baywatch* with your boyfriend as he ogles the babes?).

4. Keep a chart of your progress, as you increase your exercise routine and if you lose any weight. Seeing the results on paper (maybe even graphing it) can be inspiring.

Sound Body, Sound Mind

Research in recent years has shown that regular aerobic exercise goes a long way toward helping you to establish mood stability. Feelings of stress, anxiety, and depression can be alleviated by a vigorous exercise regimen. In fact, a single session of aerobic exercise can decrease anxiety for more than two hours.

Aerobic exercise, in addition to benefitting your health overall, which, in and of itself, alleviates stress, also boosts the levels of certain neurotransmitters in the brain. These chemicals are responsible for the "runner's high," that feeling of euphoria that some runners experience after thirty minutes of exercise.

Aerobic exercise is also a good way to give yourself a personal "time-out" from a stress-filled day. Whether you're running, swimming, or working out on a machine, it's your time (and those headphones really help to shut out the world for a while, don't they?). By distracting you from your troubles, exercise gives you a change to refuel and recharge so that you can cope better when you're confronted with those reality issues again.

REST AND RELAXATION

We live in a society in which people drive themselves hard. Part of it is the need to stay on top of things economically, but part of it is a culture that fosters workaholism. The average American worker takes far less vacation than his or her counterparts in other Western nations, and the eight-hour day has been stretched considerably by the use of home computers and laptops, which make people feel that they should be working all the time. The result is that too many of us are getting frazzled, harried, and chronically fatigued.

Rest is just as essential a component of good health as proper nutrition and exercise. About a hundred years ago, Thomas Edison invented the light bulb and radically changed people's sleeping habits. Whereas previously people went to bed at night because doing otherwise was impractical, suddenly it was possible to ignore the body's natural rhythms and stay awake until all hours. The result? Less and less rest as we play the never-ending catch-up game on sleep.

Scientists have shown that our bodies operate according to **circadian rhythms**, an inner time clock that roughly matches the twenty-four-hour cycle of night and day. Left to their own devices, most people will go to sleep when their body temperature is falling and they'll sleep for seven to eight hours. If you go to sleep when your body temperature is at its peak—let's say in the middle of the day after a big holiday feast—you would tend to sleep much longer, up to fifteen hours if left uninterrupted. So the time of day you go to sleep, not how long you've been awake, is the major determinant in how long you sleep.

Consequently, people with irregular schedules—airline pilots, medical interns, emergency relief workers—often suffer from sleep problems and deep fatigue (doesn't that make you feel great about flying?).

To feel genuinely good and to be able to perform at your peak level, you need to adhere to regular sleep habits. Most people require eight hours of sleep a night; some function well enough on six; few manage on less than that. If you are a poor sleeper, consider these suggestions to improve your sleeping habits:

- Follow a regular schedule for sleeping and waking up, even on weekends.
- Exercise regularly (but not too close to bedtime).
- Don't eat or drink anything with caffeine after midday. That includes coffee, tea, cola drinks, and chocolate.
- Before bedtime, do whatever it is that relaxes you. Read, listen to music, indulge in a hot bath. TV is a less desirable option, as it tends to stimulate the viewer.
- Avoid alcoholic beverages before bed. They may help you fall asleep, but they will wind up interfering with your sleep patterns.
- Don't worry about not sleeping. If you have trouble falling asleep, get up and do something boring until you feel sleepy.

SUBSTANCE ABUSE

You haven't gotten this far in life without having heard a great deal about substance abuse, so we're not going to take a lot of your time going over well-worn material. However, we do feel we have to give the topic some space as part of the "holistic approach" we've been presenting.

Every day we hear about athletes, movie stars, businessmen, politicians and, as they say, "people from all walks of life" who have drug problems. It's epidemic. Why do people use such harmful substances? For a variety of reasons. Some feel that it is a requirement in order to be part of a social scene. Others use drugs to "relax" themselves and take them away from their problems. Some people are just seriously into "experimentation." Whatever the reason, most drug abusers suffer from poor self-belief and a lack of confidence. They use drugs to boost their feelings about themselves. It's a bad choice, however, because drugs—whether it be alcohol, tobacco, or narcotics—are habit-forming, if not physically then psychologically.

Tobacco

As we now tragically know, one of the worst substances ever inflicted on the public is tobacco, which contains nicotine, a stimulant that increases brain activity and other bodily functions. Nicotine is a disaster. It raises blood pressure, makes the heart beat faster, and leads to acute physical and psychological dependence. When smokers try to give up nicotine (one of the world's most addictive drugs), they often experience irritability, headaches, anxiety, depression, and powerful nicotine cravings.

The statistics on mortality traced to tobacco are staggering. More people have died of smoking in this century than in all the world wars combined. Smoking is the major cause of cancer of the lungs, mouth, and throat and it contributes to heart disease and respiratory problems. Second-hand smoke—the smoke from other people's cigarettes—is a killer as well.

Smoking used to be everywhere—a staple of the American culture, from Humphrey Bogart to Bette Davis to G.I. Joe. In fact, back in 1965, about 42 percent of Americans smoked. Today smoking is banned in most offices, government buildings, schools, airplanes, and increasingly in restaurants. People who smoke now feel stigmatized and have difficulty actually finding places to smoke. In fact, smoking, except among teenagers, is on the decline, down to 25 percent of all Americans; but it is still a major national health problem.

Most people who quit smoking manage to do so on their own. It is no weakness, however, to seek outside help with your smoking problem. Talk to your doctor about a nicotine patch. Check in with organizations like Smoke Enders and the American Cancer Society. Consider hypnosis or other behavioral modification programs. You can stop, but, better yet, never start!

Alcohol

The current estimate of Americans who are addicted to alcohol ranges from 10 to 20 million. Alcohol abuse costs American business billions of dollars a year in lost productivity.

Unlike tobacco, which is a stimulant, alcohol is a depressant, decreasing brain activity and lowering blood pressure. Problem drinkers become physically and psychologically addicted to alcohol and when it is mixed with other drugs, it can be deadly. Even a few beers a day can cause liver damage over the long run, and the cost in lives and property from drunken driving is devastating.

People who have tried to stop drinking have found the most success with support groups like Alcoholics Anonymous. AA, as it is known, gets drinkers to focus on their problems, abstain totally from alcohol, and draw on the support of others in their situation.

Other Drugs

Heroin, cocaine (or crack, as it is known when smoked), amphetamines, sedatives, and tranquilizers are all deadly drugs and medical intervention and supervision is required to deal with these addictions. Marijuana is a milder drug, mostly used recreationally, but it too can have negative effects. Like alcohol, it upsets the body's coordination and reflexes and makes driving a car or operating machinery a potentially dangerous activity. Because it is smoked, it also harms the lungs.

Yet another group of drugs that is often abused are steroids. Anabolic steroid is a synthetic form of the male hormone, testosterone. Because the drug increases the body's ability to turn protein into muscle, steroids are popular among athletes. Experts say that steroid users face side effects and risks that are not yet fully understood. Women risk changes in their sexual characteristics, including shrinking of the breasts, growth of body hair, baldness, and a deepened voice. Some men suffer high blood pressure, lowered sperm counts, and acute acne. In addition, steroids seem to be as addictive as alcohol or nicotine.

Treating Drug Abuse

Recovering from drug addiction is a long-term process with three stages.

Stage 1: Wanting to Stop. Motivation is the key to Stage 1. People wanting to stop drug use must learn to trust, love, and respect themselves.

Stage 2: Stopping. During this stage it is critical for drug users to distance themselves from the drug. That may mean distancing themselves from the people (even spouses and lovers) and circumstances associated with that drug use.

Stage 3: Staying stopped. During the period of recovery, a support group will prove essential. Support groups are available all over the country to help recovering addicts stay off drugs, no matter what the drug is they are using.

If you or someone you know needs treatment for drug abuse, call the National Institute for Drug Abuse at their hotline number 1-800-662-HELP. They will refer you to programs in your immediate area.

SEXUALLY TRANSMITTED DISEASES

The last aspect of "the whole you" we will discuss is a very private aspect and has to do with your sexual activity. Sexual pleasure can be a very gratifying part of life but it is important to be aware of the sexually transmitted diseases (STD) that can come with unprotected sex. These diseases are widespread and are not limited to any specific portions of the population. The most common STDs are gonorrhea, chlamydia, and genital herpes.

Gonorrhea is an infection of the genital mucous membranes. In men, symptoms are painful urination with a discharge of pus. In women, the symptoms are mild or undetectable. Untreated gonorrhea can lead to sterility in both sexes. The good news is that gonorrhea can be cured with antibiotics.

Chlamydia is an infection of the genital and urinary tracts. It is the most widespread of the STDs, with symptoms similar to those of gonorrhea, although milder. Chlamydia can be treated with antibiotics. Left untreated, it can lead to severe pelvic inflammatory diseases in women and sterility in both men and women.

Genital herpes is caused by a virus similar to that which causes cold sores and fever blisters. The first symptoms are a tingling in the genital area and small, sometimes itchy, blisters. Genital herpes flare up periodically, with stress seeming to aggravate the condition. Although it cannot be cured, there are drugs that control the symptoms and reduce the number of relapses of the disease.

Two grave diseases transmitted through sexual activity are syphilis and AIDS. *Syphilis* is a highly infectious STD caused by a bacterium. The first symptom is a small hard sore in the genital area, mouth, or anus. By the time this symptom has appeared, the syphilis infection has already spread to the blood. Left untreated, syphilis causes fever, sore throat, headache, and sores. The disease then seems to disappear, sometimes for years, only to reappear, in the final stages, with blindness, paralysis, insanity, and ultimately death. Syphilis can be treated with antibiotics, but any damage that has already occurred cannot be reversed.

AIDS (Acquired Immune Deficiency Syndrome) is a group of twenty-nine diseases or conditions resulting from the gradual destruction of a person's immune system. A person infected with the human immunodeficiency virus (HIV) gradually loses T-cells and so becomes unable to fight off disease and dies. The time between infection with HIV and the onset of AIDS can vary from one to two years to over a decade. Although AIDS is usually transmitted sexually, it can also be transmitted through contact with blood (by sharing needles or by accident) or passed from an infected mother to her baby.

If you have reason to believe you have a sexually transmitted disease, go to a doctor or clinic immediately. In addition, pregnant women with a history of STDs should inform their doctor, since some diseases are passed from mother to child. The best strategy for dealing with STDs is prevention. The spread of these diseases can be stopped through the practice of "safe sex" using condoms or celibacy. The latter is gaining in popularity among the young, who are finding ways to experience satisfying sexual release without direct sexual contact.

READY, SET, ABLE

Now that you've reviewed the "whole you," and looked at yourself and your lifestyle with a holistic approach, you're ready to take stock and move on to other aspects of your life as a student. Your relationship to others in your world seems a good next stop.

ROUTE FIVE

WELCOME TO THE WORLD: HOW DO YOU FIT IN?

KEY TERMS

body language
communication barriers
responsiveness
assertiveness
mirroring
open-ended questions

By virtue of the fact that you are sitting here in cosmetology school, we'll go out on a limb and make certain assumptions about you. We'll wager that you are artistically oriented with quite a bit of that Visual-Spatial Intelligence we talked about in our Route 3 chapter. You are good with your hands, possessing a tactile sensitivity that makes it pleasurable for you to run your fingers through someone's hair. We also suspect that you are drawn to entrepreneurial pursuits and perhaps dream about owning your own salon one day. Finally, we have a hunch that you are something of a people person. Even though you may be quiet and would never call yourself the life of the party, you understand that in your chosen line of work you are going to be thrown together with all kinds of people all day long: co-workers and customers. You're going to have to find a way of getting along with them, communicating with them, and even enjoying them. So let's have a look at the ways people interact with each other, and, more to the point, the ways that those interactions can be improved.

ARE WE HAVING A COMMUNICATION PROBLEM?

That's what the warden kept asking in the classic Paul Newman prison film *Cool Hand Luke*, but the fact is that people have communication problems all the time. The good news is that communication is a skill that can be developed and honed, so that the problems recede and the successes come to the forefront.

What is communication anyway? Basically, it is an exchange of messages. The messages can be verbal, using spoken or written words—a face-to-face conversation, a phone conversation, letters, or email—or they can be nonverbal, as in gestures, facial expressions, and body language. For communication to occur, there needs to be a *sender*, who transmits the message, and a *receiver*, to whom the message is sent. Effective communication occurs when sender and receiver are in sync and both have a clear understanding of what the message is all about.

Communication comes in two forms: *one-way communications* and *two-way communications*. In one-way communication, the sender sends and the receiver receives without returning another message. Example: your teacher lectures, you receive (and hopefully write down some notes). Another example: Your mother yells at you for leaving wet towels on the bathroom floor and she doesn't want to hear one word back from you. To keep the peace, you keep your mouth shut. End of conversation.

In two-way communication, the sender transmits a message, the receiver gets it, and the receiver responds with another message. Example: Your teacher lectures, you ask a relevant question, your teacher responds. Example: Your mother yells at you for leaving wet towels on the bathroom floor. You respond that your little sister left them there. Your mother takes off after your little sister.

Nonverbal Communications

Spoken communications are the tip of the iceberg when it comes to communications as a whole. The entire repertoire of our nonverbal communications make up the bulk of how we exchange information with each other. In fact, studies show that 80 to 90 percent of the impact of a message comes from nonverbal elements—facial expressions, eye contact, body language, and tone of voice.

Nonverbal communication can be much more revealing than verbal communication, so it is important to pay attention to the signs that people give off nonverbally. Primarily they are delivered in the following ways:

Facial Expressions. A smile, a frown, a pout, a knit brow, the raising of eyebrows—the human face is remarkably mobile, capable of producing literally thousands of movements. Some facial expressions are universal (a frown in Boston is the same as a frown in Bombay). The intensity and frequency of facial expressions may, however, vary from culture to culture. In Italy, people may be highly demonstrative when it comes to facial expressions, while in Sweden facial expressions may be more subtle or veiled.

Most of us have no trouble drawing impressions from other people's facial expressions. Sadness, anger, hostility, excitement, and happiness are all quickly decoded. We may have more trouble, however, when it comes to judging character from facial expressions. A ready smile does not necessarily mean that a person is really warm or to be trusted.

Eye Contact. In some cultures, looking downward while speaking to someone is received as a sign of respect. In the United States, however, if you were to look downward while on a job interview, your prospective employer might decide you are withdrawn or shifty. So, while you're on these shores, make sure you establish good eye contact with the person with whom you are communicating.

Body Language. If you have ever followed politicians in an election year, you could do a quick study on the subject of **body language**. Some politicians, like Senator John McCain, move comfortably around a stage and are able to immediately establish rapport with an audience. Others, like Vice President Albert Gore, have a tendency to hold themselves stiffly and formally and must "relearn" body language in order to make an effective impression on voters.

All of us have to be aware of our body language when we are trying to make positive impressions on people. Tension in our bodies can make communication tense, and overgesticulation can act as a turn-off. It's also important to observe an appropriate distance between yourself and your receiver in a communication. In mainstream U.S. culture, people who are lovers, close family members, or intimate friends are comfortable standing about a foot apart. Acquaintances or colleagues, however, usually stand four to twelve feet apart when communicating.

Voice Qualities. Pay attention to how your voice sounds when you're communicating (or have a cooperative receiver provide you with feedback on the subject). Is your voice loud or soft, high or low pitched, fast or slow? Is the tone pleasant or harsh or monotonous?

Whatever your voice qualities are, they can be altered for a more positive impression. If you speak very quickly, for instance, you can make a conscious effort to slow yourself down, enlisting friends and family to alert you to when you're falling into your "speedtalk" mode.

EXERCISE 5-1: Observing Nonverbal Communication

Try the following activity, which will improve your awareness of nonverbal communication. Have a conversation with a classmate or friend and pay close attention to nonverbal communication. Write down what you observed in the space provided.

1. What facial expressions did you notice?
   _____
   _____

2. Did you maintain eye contact throughout the conversation? If not, when was eye contact broken?
   _____

3. What body postures, head movements, and gestures did you notice?
   _____
   _____

4. Describe the person's voice.
   Volume _____
   Pitch _____
   Speed _____
   Tone _____

BARRIERS TO COMMUNICATION

It would be a wonderful world if all our communications were open, easy, and meaningful, but that's not the way human interactions work, unfortunately. There are a number of factors that inhibit or complicate communication. Let's look at some of these **communication barriers**, all in the context of a networking cocktail party you're attending with an eye toward making contacts that might lead to some job information.

Physical Barriers. Cocktail parties can be a minefield of physical barriers. For one thing, the noise level ranges from high to deafening. For another thing, you might find yourself in an awkward position, jammed into a corner. People naturally form into clusters at such gatherings and sometimes it can take quite an intrepid individual to "break into" the circle.

Mental Barriers. For many people, the idea of going into a room full of strangers is a particularly horrible form of torture. Uncomfortable in such a situation, your mind may start blowing out of proportion all the things you fancy are wrong with you: you're awkward, you're tongue-tied, you're boring, whatever. This is a time for some positive self-talk, as we discussed in our Route Two chapter.

Another mental barrier that might inhibit communication is dealing with *selective attention*, either your own or your receiver's. Either one of you may be unable to keep yourself from scanning the room, looking for fresh faces or some other exciting circles to join. This, obviously, does nothing for eye contact.

A third mental barrier might have to do with choice of words. The person with whom you are communicating, for instance, may be using industry jargon that means nothing to you yet, and you may not feel secure enough to ask for clarification. Your conversation, therefore, becomes a nonverbal one, in which you are nodding emptily until you can excuse yourself for another glass of sparkling water (alcoholic beverages may initially loosen up your conversational talents, but, before you can say "Jack Daniels," a lot of your articulation and focus may go down the chute).

Emotional Barriers. Any number of emotional barriers may enter into this cocktail party picture. You may have just gotten bad news—your car needs a new transmission; it will cost $3,000 and you have $800 in the bank—and your mind is more on that than the conversations at hand.

There can be other emotionally-charged issues. If you are African-American in a predominantly white group, you may have issues around that. If you are disabled, you bring a whole other set of feelings to such a gathering. If you're the oldest or youngest person in the room, that's fraught with emotional baggage as well.

Cultural Barriers. If you are originally from another culture, the cultural traditions, manners, and habits you bring with you may initially create distance for you in the speaker-listener relationship. You may come from a culture, for instance, in which deference is readily shown, as in bowing, and this may be misinterpreted when you find yourself in the United States. An attentive eye to those around you and an open mind and resolution to move beyond your own ethnic group will help with this issue.

Lack of Rapport. Perhaps the most common inhibitor to meaningful conversation in such a context is the fact that the person you're speaking with just doesn't do it for you (or you for him). There's no chemistry there. You find him a stuffed shirt, a flake, a snob, a blowhard. That's the time for you to pull out a few conversational gambits to ease you out of a sticky situation (e.g. "I'm just going to refresh my drink"; "I just have to visit the ladies' room"; "Will you excuse me? I just spotted an old friend").

Communication Styles

One key to success as a communicator is to recognize the type of communication style you possess, and to be aware of the communication styles of others. In other words, you should have a sense of who you are as a communicator, and you should be comfortable with your style.

Researchers David Merrill and Roger Reid discovered that people essentially show two major forms of behavior when they communicate: responsiveness and assertiveness. **Responsiveness** is the degree to which a person is open in his or her dealings with others. Someone with a low degree of responsiveness may be guarded or even quite closed to interactions with others. On the other hand, someone with a high degree of responsiveness will readily show emotion and will almost always be perceived by others as being friendly. **Assertiveness** suggests behavior ranging from asking questions (low assertiveness) to telling others what is expected of them (high assertiveness).

These two modes of communication styles can be combined in a diagram, as shown in Figure 5-1. By placing the two behaviors of responsiveness and assertiveness

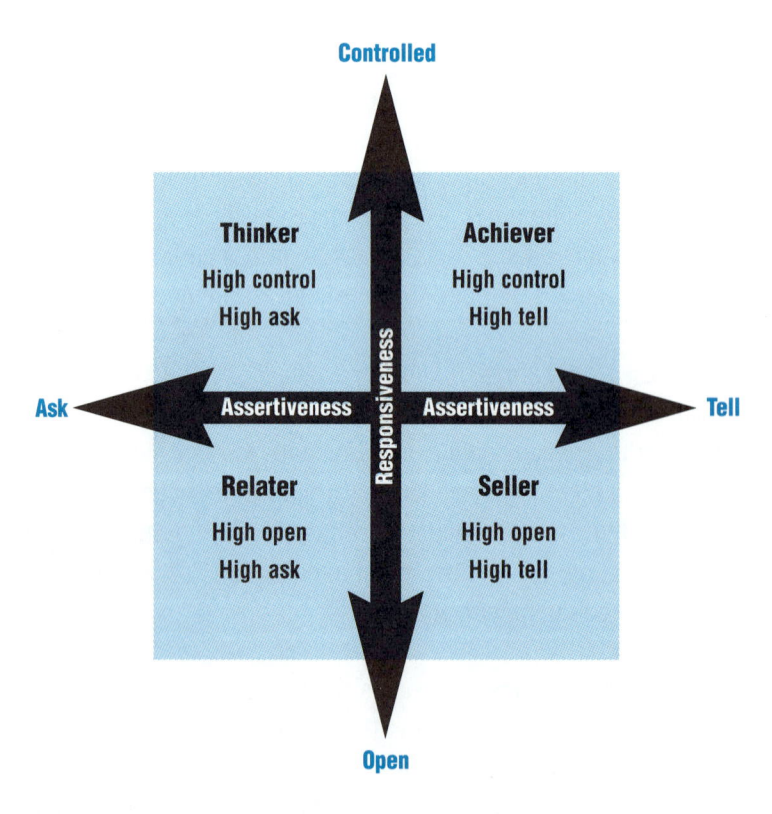

Controlled

	Thinker	Achiever
	High control	High control
	High ask	High tell

Ask ← Assertiveness | Assertiveness → Tell

(Responsiveness)

	Relater	Seller
	High open	High open
	High ask	High tell

Open

FIGURE 5-1

at right angles to each other, we come up with a model with four boxes. A person's degree of responsiveness and assertiveness will place him or her in one of the boxes, each of which correlates to a communication style: Thinker, Achiever, Seller, and Relater. Have a look and then decide which kind you are.

- **The Thinker.** Thinkers are people who tend to be guarded in their interactions with others. They are not hale-fellow-well-met, slap-you-on-the-back types. Self-control is very important to them and they generally are very reserved when it comes to revealing personal information. Instead, they choose to deflect attention from themselves by asking questions of those with whom they are communicating.

- **The Achiever.** Like Thinkers, Achievers score high in the self-control department and resist the impulse to reveal much about their inner selves. Unlike Thinkers, however, Achievers are very assertive people. They do not hesitate to express their expectations clearly.

- **The Seller.** The Seller is a "people" person. Touchy, feely, warm, and outgoing with others, he or she is also assertive and given to forthright expression, often telling you about his or her accomplishments and ambitions.

- **The Relater.** Relaters are usually warm and friendly in their interactions with others. They are less concerned about themselves than they are about their receivers. Relaters ask questions which are sometimes quite personal in nature.

Understanding the Communication Styles

Most of us incorporate some aspects from several of the above types. For example, when you communicate with a close friend or spouse, you may be very open and personal, as in the style of a Relater. When you communicate with your boss, however, you may be very self-controlled and unassertive, as in the case of the Thinker. In general, however, over time, each of us tends to favor one style in most of our interactions with others.

EXERCISE 5-2 What Is Your Communication Style?

Find out what your dominant communication style is by checking off each of the communication characteristics that apply to you. The box with the most check marks represents your preferred communication style.

Thinker	**Achiever**
__ Quiet, level tone of voice	__ Factual speech
__ Leans back or away	__ Leans forward and faces others
__ Limited eye contact	__ Limited facial expressions
__ Stiff posture	__ Limited body movements
__ Uses big words	__ Fast-paced speech
Relater	**Seller**
__ Little emphasis on detail	__ Dramatic or loud tone of voice
__ Touches others	__ Animated facial expressions
__ Smiles, nods	__ Direct eye contact
__ Casual posture	__ Lots of body and hand motions
__ Talks about relationships	__ Uses voice to emphasize points

EFFECTIVE COMMUNICATION

Our goal as people out in the world is to achieve a high level of successful communication. This makes our jobs easier and our opportunities more plentiful. A good sense of the different communication styles described above will help in this task.

Inevitably and frequently, people whose communication styles do not mesh well are thrown together. As a result, they can expect friction or, at best, distance...unless they learn some useful ways of coping with and overcoming communications gaps.

Let's take the example of Julie, a Seller, and Loretta, a Thinker, both of whom work in the same salon. Loretta has been assigned to train Julie, and they are having problems. Basically, they don't speak the same language and therefore they don't relate very well. But Julie needs to make this work, so here's what she does.

Julie decides that she will study and imitate Loretta's communication style. This is a process called **mirroring**, and it is one of the most valuable skills you can learn. Now most people do a certain amount of mirroring without even being consciously aware of it. If you watch two people deep in conversation, you'll see that their postures are often similar or that they're both speaking softly. This kind of unconscious mirroring can, however, become a conscious device for you to use again and again in your interactions with people. Keep in mind that mirroring does not mean imitation so obvious that the other person becomes aware of it. Rather, mirroring consists of small, subtle adjustments in your communication behavior to more closely match your conversational partner. When you mirror successfully, the other person feels that you are in harmony. People are most comfortable with those they think are like themselves.

Your mirroring can be achieved with body movements—crossing your legs when your opposite does; folding your arms—or by responding in kind to her smiles, nods, and other aspects of her body language. Again, remember that you don't want to come off as an imitator. Your mirroring must be subtle or it can become downright offensive.

You can also mirror your receiver by matching his or her use of words. A person's vocabulary is often characterized by a particular reliance on one of the five senses. Visual people say things like "I'll watch out for that" or "It's clear to me." Hearing-connected people use phrases like "That rings a bell" or "I hear what you're saying." Those who favor the sense of touch will use expressions like "This feels right" or "I can't get a hold of it." See if you can figure out what "sense pattern" your conversational partner is using and try mirroring it.

EXERCISE 5-3 Say It Again

How could you say the same thing to three different people who prefer different senses for perception? Rewrite the question, "What do you think it means?" using words that each person might choose.

1. Visual person:
   _____
   _____

2. Auditory (hearing) person
   _____
   _____

3. Feeling (touching) person
   _____
   _____

LISTEN UP

Now that we've talked about different styles of communication, we need to look at the mechanics of communication. This basically breaks down into two functions: listening and speaking. Of the two, listening often requires considerably more practice before you get good at it.

We've all been in the position of telling a friend, a family member, or a co-worker some important news—we got a bad review at work; we're breaking up with someone; we got rear-ended stopped at a traffic light—and as we're telling this news, we suddenly realize that friend/family member/co-worker *isn't even listening!*

We can't afford to be too self-righteous about this because we've been guilty of the same offense ourselves. It's called a breakdown in communication and it can be damaging to a relationship. It can also be costly in a work context. "If each of America's more than 100 million workers prevented just one $10 mistake by better listening, their organizations would gain over $1 billion in profits," says Lyman K. Steil, president of Communication Development Inc., a consulting firm that teaches listening skills (Harris, 1989). So why is listening so hard, and what can we do to improve our skills?

Do You Hear Me?

Listening certainly seems easy enough. You keep your ears open, words are said, a conversation occurs. But listening goes way beyond simple hearing. To listen effectively, you need to use not just your ears, but your brain. And you need to listen with concentration, which means tuning out the hundreds of other things that are going on around you as well as those in your head. Chief among these obstacles are:

Distractions. That cocktail party situation is a good example of the kind of distractions that can derail a conversation. A lot of people in the room, loud music, the fact that the person you're conversing with is wearing an overwhelming perfume or has a peculiar tic or is wearing a dress with a neckline that plunges down to Florida...there are always distractions a-plenty.

Preconceptions. All kinds of preconceptions cloud our accessibility and openness to good, useful conversations. We may be laboring under the conviction that women with bleached blond hair and lots of makeup don't have anything serious to say. We may be unconsciously discriminating against elderly people, and feel that anyone over the age of 70 doesn't need to be listened to with any real attention. You may be discriminating against people under the age of 17 for the same reason. In any case, you're losing opportunities to hear something of interest if you let your preconceptions rule you.

Self-Absorption. A common pitfall in meaningful dialogue between two parties occurs when one party is so absorbed with his or her own agenda that the speaker is being tuned out. Instead of listening carefully to the other person, the listener (or should we say "non-listener") is busy planning and rehearsing his or her response. Essentially, the whole time is spent with the listener keeping an ear out for when he or she can jump in and dominate the conversation.

Daydreaming. Have you ever fallen into a mental "black hole" during a conversation? Something in the room—a poster perhaps—has you thinking of a ski trip you once took to Utah and you're overtaken with the memory of schussing down a slope. This kind of daydreaming occurs because the brain can process words much faster than the speaker can say them. Your brain deals with this down time by filling it with daydreams...daydreams that are often so intoxicating they're hard to free yourself from them.

Doing a Better Job at Listening

By following a few simple pointers and by viewing listening as a genuine learning experience, you can reap some real benefits in terms of the connectedness you'll achieve with other people. Give up your passive listening style, filled with meaningless nods and murmured "Uh-huhs" and, in their place, substitute an active listening style in which you are concentrating on the speaker and are participating in the communication.

There is a range of techniques you can learn in order to become a more active and effective listener. These techniques include being physically prepared, being open to the other person, being curious, asking questions, and listening for the meaning of the words and the unspoken message.

Be Physically Prepared. If you're finding that a lot of conversations seem to pass right over your head, you might start by asking yourself if you have some kind of hearing deficit. Before you dismiss this as absurd, keep in mind that it is not just older people who have hearing problems. A lot of younger people who work around heavy machinery or who are in the habit of listening to loud music on headphones do have a quantifiable hearing deficit. If you find out that you do, there are all kinds of amazing technologies available today to compensate for routine hearing deficits.

You can also maximize your ability to hear by situating yourself in environments or locations that are more conducive to good listening. In a classroom environment, for instance, sit close to the speaker so you can hear well. (You might get called on more frequently, but if you've been listening, that shouldn't be a problem!) You should also be able to see the speaker, for your sense of sight enhances your sense of hearing. Watching the speaker's nonverbal cues helps clue you in to what he or she is talking about.

Be Open. The Japanese symbol for the word "listen" shows the character for "ear" placed within the character for "gate." When we listen to someone, we are in effect passing through the other person's gate and entering his or her world. To do this, we have to get ourselves into an open, nonjudging place...which can often be easier said than done.

To be open to another person means that you risk having your feelings, ideas, or attitudes changed. This is not to say that you have to agree with everything the speaker says. Rather, you just have to subscribe to the principle that others have the right to say what they want to say and you would do well to keep an open mind to what it is they're saying.

Concisely put, it means that you open yourself up to receiving a communication and then you evaluate it, not before the fact.

Be Curious. Curiosity killed the cat, goes the old adage, but you know what? Curiosity doesn't kill listeners. A curious listener is liable to find out a lot of interesting information. So let your curiosity overcome any knee-jerk tendency to be judgmental and go with the flow.

Ask Questions. There are very few circumstances in which the word "passive" is regarded as a positive attribute, and listening is no exception. The passive listener is usually in that position because he's bored, insecure, is not paying attention, or is not open to other people. You can slough off your passivity by taking an active part in a conversation through the pointed asking of questions. Effective listeners ask questions in a way that will elicit information, and they will go away much the richer for the exchange.

In general, the most effective questions are those we call **open-ended questions**. Open-ended questions are the opposite of questions that can be answered with a "yes" or "no." Barbara Walters does not ask the celebrity she is interviewing if he or she would like to be an oak tree ("No, Barbara. I wouldn't."). Rather, she asks them what kind of tree they would like to be ("A weeping willow, Barbara, because I have so much sadness in my heart."). As a rule, questions beginning with *Who, What, Where, When, Why,* and *How* are open-ended questions (e.g. "What happened in the meeting?", "How did you feel when you lost your first job?", "Why did you marry so late?" and so on). Close-ended questions are useful, however, when you want an answer that is absolutely clear. You might, for instance, ask your professor, "Is our paper due on March 16?" and he will say either "Yes" or "No"—no confusion.

EXERCISE 5-4 Asking Good Questions

For each of the following items, write a question that will elicit the response indicated. Then say whether the question is open-ended or close-ended.

1. Question: _____

   _____

   Response: The coat is black with a leather belt.

   Type of question: _____

2. Question: _____

   _____

   Response: He makes me uncomfortable because he gives me orders rather than asking me to do something.

   Type of question: _____

3. Question: _____

   _____

   Response: I like the red one better.

   Type of question: _____

4. Question: _____
   _____

   Response: First we decided what type of playground we wanted, then we made a plan, and finally we enlisted other people to help us build it.
   Type of question: _____

5. Question: _____
   _____

   Response: No, I don't like it.
   Type of question: _____

Listening for Meaning and Verbal Cues

We mentioned above how the speed of the brain's processing creates conditions wherein the listener is liable to lapse into daydreaming. Those conditions, when the brain is waiting for that next input from the speaker, can be used more productively if the listener uses it to think about the meaning of what is being said.

As you listen to the speaker's words, test out your critical thinking skills (see Route 3: It's All in the Mind) and try to identify the ideas, the facts, and the relationship between them. Ask yourself: What is the most important thing being said here? What facts or ideas support the main idea? Is there cause and effect? Is a time sequence involved? Is this a fact or an opinion you're hearing? Thinking critically about the message *while you're hearing the message* will help you understand it and will keep your attention focused on the communication at hand.

This process will also set you up for cues as to your own responses. For example, if you are being interviewed for a job, pay careful attention to what the interviewer is saying. If he talks a lot about the company's reputation for high quality service, you can respond by citing the time you worked at an airline counter for a summer and received a citation for your excellent service. If the interviewer asks an open-ended question (and interviewers are trained to ask such questions), be prepared to answer with a response of some weight or complexity and make sure to avoid "yes" or "no" answers unless it is entirely clear that they would suffice. For example, if an interviewer asks whether you would consider relocation, a simple "yes" will not do. A better response would be, "I am prepared to go wherever I need to in order to get the kind of satisfying work I'm seeking. In fact, I look forward to the opportunity to live in different locations while I still have the flexibility in my life to make those kinds of changes."

Listen Between the Lines

Paying attention to the words of a speaker alone is not enough to qualify as a complete listening experience. An active listener also makes sure to focus on nonverbal cues. As we have said, a whole battery of nonverbal indicators—eye contact, facial expressions, voice quality, and body language—contribute to the message being delivered. By paying attention to these nonverbal cues, you can learn a great deal more from your listening experience.

Most nonverbal communication cues are visual, so make a point of having the speaker be in your line of vision. Then become a student of the drama of human expression, and learn what an arched eyebrow, the bitten corner of a lip, a clenched jaw, a wink or a brisk nod are all about. (Of course, there are probably thousands of subtle gestures, so keep up your observations!)

Taking Notes

If you need to be a really serious listener—let's say, you're in a lecture or you're receiving instructions on how to get somewhere or how to operate a tool—you'll want to move your listening into a high-end mode and start taking some notes. Taking notes forces you to pay attention to what's being said and ensures that messages will not have to be repeated. If you are in the position of listening to a busy, important person, nothing will alienate that person more quickly than your asking them to take precious time out of their schedule to repeat what they've already told you.

EXERCISE 5-5 Fact or Opinion?

Distinguishing between fact and opinion is important for effective listening. Indicate whether each of the following statements is a fact or an opinion.

1. You don't need reservations to eat dinner at that restaurant. _____

2. The food there is pretty good. _____

3. The last time we had dinner there, the waiter spilled coffee on the table. _____

4. I thought the chocolate sundae was too sweet. _____

5. The bill came to $29 without the tip. _____

SPEAK AND THEY SHALL LISTEN

Your speech is made up of a lot more than just the words you choose. You might have the world's most elegant vocabulary, but if you slur your words or shout them, no one's going to care. In studies of face-to-face communication, Dr. Albert Mehrabian has found that the impact on the listener of the speaker's appearance and voice is far greater than the impact of the speaker's words (Figure 5-2). In fact, since listeners see you before they hear you, your appearance has a great effect on your ability to get your message across. Experts say that you have between seven and ten seconds to make that crucial good first impression.

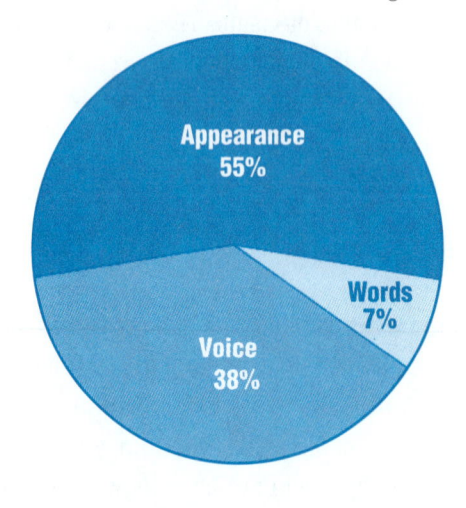

FIGURE 5-2

In other words, neatness counts. Good posture and clean, conservative dress are important for making that first impression (unless you're auditioning for a rock band). Wild body piercings and outrageous hair colors are going to reduce your chances of connecting with the widest range of people, and this could be costly if you're going on job interviews. If your greatest priority in life is to roll out of bed every morning, run a brush through your hair and slip on a Grateful Dead T-shirt, you might have to organize your life around that priority and instead of becoming a bank teller, you would go to work in a record shop.

Speech Qualities

Fran Drescher, a.k.a. The Nanny, did perfectly all right for herself with her diamond-cutting voice, but most people are going to have a harder time going through life with a voice like that. Most of us have to pay some attention at least to issues like volume (too soft is as bad as too loud—remember the *Seinfeld* episode about "low speakers"?); the speed of one's words (funereal slowness or rapid-fire diction can both be turnoffs); and correct usage of English grammar. All of these are important factors in how we present ourselves to the world.

In the United States, there are four basic varieties of spoken American English: standard English, dialects, accented English, and substandard English.

- *Standard English* is the English you hear spoken by national news broadcasters, actors, and others who have rid themselves of regional or social dialects.

- *Dialects* are variations of American English spoken in particular geographical areas or by particular social groups. Boston has its "chowdah," New York has its "New Yawk," the South has its "Y'all." Ebonics, a dialect spoken by many African Americans, is found in all regions of the United States.

- *Accented English* is spoken by many Americans for whom English is an acquired or second language.

- *Substandard English* is English spoken with poor pronunciation, enunciation, grammar, and vocabulary. "Liberry" for "library" and "ain't got none" for "don't have any" are examples of substandard English.

If you are aiming to speak to the largest cross section of the population—if, for instance, you are attempting to become a national news broadcaster—you would closely study the speech habits of a Tom Brokaw or a Diane Sawyer in order to acquire their habits of Standard English. If you are planning to stay within a particular regional or social grouping—if, for instance, you were planning to work in a beauty salon that catered to African-Americans—you could feel confident that your use of ebonics would not inhibit your career progress.

Volume, Pitch, Rate, and Tone

A pleasant, even tone of voice will open many doors for you...or at least may keep doors from being shut in your face. The volume of your voice refers to its intensity or loudness. If you are always speaking as if you're playing to the last row in the balcony, you may notice people shying away from you. Similarly, if you mumble or swallow your words, people may soon tire of saying "Pardon?" or "Did you say something?" and will find the next opportunity to slip away from you. Good speech volume has a lot to do with breath control, so you might want to breathe deeply and control your breath as singers and actors do.

Pitch refers to the level of sound on a musical scale. People who speak with a high-pitched voice sound shrill and unappealing. Moderate pitch is what most speakers strive for.

Issues around rate of speech vary depending on what part of the country in which you find yourself. In the South, people are used to conversation that can strike Northerners as molasses-slow. On the other hand, a Southerner in New York might soon get lost in the typical rapid-fire exchange that characterizes the Big Apple. Rate, like volume and pitch, is most attractive when modulated. You can slow down to emphasize important facts and speed up when you're dealing with relatively inconsequential information. Make sure, however, to avoid filling your pauses with sounds like "um" or "uh." These fillers only serve to distract your listeners.

Tone is also an important aspect of speaking. Those who sound chronically depressed, whiny, unnaturally pert and chirpy, or who speak in the monotone that gives rise to the expression "monotonous" are advised to vary their tone so as not to be typed as a certain kind of personality. We all have aspects of the above characteristics in our make-up; don't let your voice convince your listener that you are one-dimensional.

Enunciation and Pronunciation

To enunciate means to speak your words clearly. Too often, "did you" becomes "didja" or "talkin'" is substituted for "talking." Addition of unnecessary sounds or syllables also characterizes poor enunciation, as in "umberella" for "umbrella" or "disasterous" for "disastrous." Ask a friend with good enunciation to keep an ear out for your mistakes and to let you know about them.

Pronunciation is closely related to enunciation. You want to make sure to correctly pronounce words, so as to make the best possible impression on your listeners. Have a look at the table below for commonly mispronounced words:

TABLE 5-1 Commonly Mispronounced Words

INCORRECT	CORRECT	INCORRECT	CORRECT
omost	almost	liberry	library
irrevelant	irrelevant	fasten	fas(t)en
probly	probably	nucular	nuclear
akst	asked	idear	idea
oways	always	sophmore	sophomore
famly	family	drownded	drowned
mischievioius	mischievous	burgular	burglar
corps	cor(p)s	often	of(t)en
jest	just	preventative	preventive

Issues of pronunciation, as well as grammar and vocabulary building, can be greatly helped by using audiotapes to build your strengths in those areas or even by enrolling in a basic course at your school or an adult education center. It is important to brush up in these areas, and on the ways you listen and speak generally, for often these skills are your passport out of and into a whole new world that is filled with all kinds of new opportunities.

REFERENCES

Harris, T. W. (1989, June). Listen carefully. *Nation's Business*, 78.

ROUTE SIX

GET A GRIP: HARMONY WITH OTHERS AND WITHIN YOURSELF

KEY TERMS

stress
coping mechanisms
behavior modification
reframing
assertiveness
Johari window
feedback
rationalization
defense mechanisms
displacement
projection

Now that you've enrolled in school, you may be experiencing a rising tide of emotions or perhaps you're even caught in a flash flood of feelings. You're excited: this is something you've always wanted to do. You're scared: you don't have the world's greatest track record when it comes it comes to finishing what you've started. You're excited: you're finally embarking on a course of action toward something concrete, something that seems to make sense. You're scared: are you up to the task or is the course you've set going to prove to be a collision course? You're excited: you're in school and, if you do what you're supposed to do, you'll wind up with a degree and a marketable skill. You're scared: this is costing a lot of money and that means working double-time, borrowing from friends and family, and cutting back on your recreational activities.

All of this may be adding up to a lot of stress and you're going to have to figure out how to handle it. Until you learn to handle that stress, it's going to be difficult for you to "work and play well with others" and your ability to do just that—interact with other people on and off the job—is going to determine to a large extent just how well you do in the world generally.

So let's take a good hard look at the subject of stress and see what we can come up with.

THE NATURE OF STRESS

Two stylists at a flourishing salon come to work one day to find out that the owner has died of a heart attack and his family is planning to close the entire operation. Both stylists are in comparable economic circumstances—each has saved enough money to buy about six month's worth of time during which they should be able to line up a new job at comparable pay, given their work history—but the two women react in totally different ways. Joan gets to work calling every one she knows and within a few days she has lined up some interviews. Patty, on the other hand, gets completely hysterical and spends all of her time moaning and groaning on the phone with her mother, her sister, and her girlfriends.

The point of this story is that different people handle stress in different ways. Many psychologists believe that stress, like beauty, is in the mind of the beholder. A situation, an event, or a change in and of itself may not be enough to cause stress. Rather, **stress** is the emotional and physical reaction that results when a person has trouble *coping* with a situation, event, or change. And, when it comes to coping, different people have different ways of coping that make certain situations harder for some to deal with than others.

Of course, there are some situations that stress out just about everyone and, when we're exposed to stress, our bodies react. We put out increased levels of adrenaline, which cause the body to produce more energy, higher blood pressure, and a faster heart rate. These responses can help us deal with stress in the short run (when a bear is chasing you, you are stressed, your adrenaline pumps, and that extra adrenaline helps get you up a tree in no time!). But when stress continues over a long period, it can be damaging to your health. Prolonged stress can contribute to heart disease and cancer; it can produce stomach ulcers, irritable bowel syndrome, colitis, migraines, and any number of other illnesses.

The psychological toll of prolonged stress can also be high. People may begin to feel that they have lost control over their lives and, consequently, they may feel helpless, anxious, and ultimately depressed. Sometimes these symptoms become so severe that they require treatment with therapy, medication, and perhaps even hospitalization.

Modern life is full of stress (in fact, life has always been full of stress; it wasn't exactly restful to be in The Crusades!) and people have to learn how to handle it. You have to understand the causes and the effects to get the big picture on stress and know how to deal with it. Let's start with the causes.

IS NOTHING GOING RIGHT?

Although different people respond to events with different degrees of stress, there are, as we've said, certain generalizations we can make about what causes stress.

- Negative events cause more stress than positive events. Planning a wedding is stressful in the sense that there are many details to attend to and people to please; but getting divorced, an essentially negative event, is far more stressful because the ramifications spill out all over a person's life.

- Unpredictable events are more stressful than predictable events. Hay fever may make a person miserable every Spring, but if it comes regularly as clockwork, a person can make some kind of adjustment and rearrange his or her life accordingly. The flu, on the other hand, is more stressful because it hits a person without warning and there are frightening implications as to where the sickness might lead.

- Uncontrollable events are more stressful than controllable events. Quitting a job is much less stressful than getting fired. Being in the driver's seat, even though it may present difficulties, helps to remedy some of the stress.

- Uncertain events are more stressful than certain events. A pop quiz creates a lot more stress in most people than an announced exam, even if the former carries less weight.

The Breaking Point

There is the usual day-to-day stress and then there are the real crunchers. Daily irritations can be very stressful—sitting in a traffic jam on a crowded commute; misplacing your keys; missing a train; having a fight with your spouse about something silly—but we come to expect things like that. As we've said, stress is built into modern life. If this kind of day-to-day stress becomes too much for you, you may have to make some changes. You might want to move out of the suburbs and into the city, where you work, if you've had it with commuting. You might want to get a sensor on your keyring that gives off a beeping noise if you're in the habit of misplacing your keys. Or you might want to develop certain techniques, like meditation (which we'll discuss in more depth a little later on) to get you past your daily irritations.

Major life events, however, can sometimes produce stress that is not so easily dealt with. In fact, too much stress can lead to "overload" situations that can actually cause illness. Psychiatrist Thomas H. Holmes and his colleagues did research on the interrelationship of major life changes, the amount of adjustment they required, and illness (Holmes & Rahe, 1967; Masuda, 1974). They found that the more major changes an individual experienced in a short time, the more likely he or she would become ill.

In their survey of 394 adults, they uncovered interesting information about how much adjustment each major life change requires. From this, they came up with the Social Readjustment Rating Scale (Table 6-1). According to this scale, the death of a spouse is the most stressful event, with a rating of 100, while minor violations of the law are the least stressful, in the 11 rating area. Holmes found that when people experience a number of major life changes within a year, they

TABLE 6-1 Social Readjustment Rating Scale

LIFE EVENT	VALUE	LIFE EVENT	VALUE
Death of spouse	100	Son or daughter leaving home	29
Divorce	73	Trouble with in-laws	29
Separation from spouse	65	Outstanding personal achievement	28
Jail term	63	Spouse begins or stops work	26
Death of close family member	63	Starting or finishing school	26
Personal injury or illness	63	Change in living conditions	25
Marriage	50	Change in personal habits	24
Fired from work	47	Trouble with boss	23
Reconciliation with spouse	45	Change in work hours or conditions	20
Retirement	45	Moving	20
Change in health of family member	44	Change in schools	20
Pregnancy	40	Change in recreational habits	19
Sex difficulties	39	Change in social activities	18
Addition to family	39	Change in sleeping habits	16
Change of financial status	38	Change in number of family gatherings	15
Death of close friend	37	Change in eating habits	15
Change of career	36	Vacation	13
Change in number of marital arguments	33	Christmas or major holiday	12
Foreclosure of mortgage or loan	30	Minor violation of the law	11
Change in work responsibilities	29		

Source: Reprinted with permission from *Journal of Psychosomatic Research*, vol. 11, p. 213, Thomas H. Holmes & Richard H. Rahe, "The Social Readjustment Rating Scale," copyright 1967, Pergamon Press plc.

are more likely to become ill. About half of the people with scores of 150 to 300, and 70 percent with scores over 300, developed an illness within a year or two.

What is interesting to learn from this scale is the idea that even major life events generally associated with good times—having a baby, getting married, and starting school (ring any bells?)—require a good deal of readjustment and can contribute significantly to your stress quotient.

★ EXERCISE 6-1 Assess Your Stress: Major Life Changes

Review the major life events in Table 6-1. How many have happened to you in the last twelve months? Write the event and its point value in the space below. Then tally up the points for an overview of just how stressed you really are.

Event	Value
_____	_____
_____	_____
_____	_____

Total value:

150 or less	Reasonable level of stress
151 to 299	Moderate stress
300 or above	Intense stress

TELLTALE SIGNS OF STRESS

How can you tell when you're "stressed out"? Let your body be your guide. You'll probably notice right off some distinct physical symptoms. These vary from person to person, but a stressed out individual could expect increased pulse rate, shortness of breath, nausea, insomnia, fatigue, muscle tension, and back or neck pain. Formerly contained habits like nail-biting or playing with one's hair may fly out of control. When stress continues, serious illness or injury may result.

Physical symptoms are almost inevitably accompanied by mood and personality changes. People suffering from stress often find themselves behaving in odd ways. They may become irritable or hostile, with extreme mood swings. Stressed out individuals have a hard time maintaining "climate control" and can veer from almost a kind of giddiness to an outlook on life that can be absolutely bleak.

When the mood goes into a downswing, it may stay down and ultimately give way to a crippling depression. Depression must not be confused with normal sadness or grief following a loss. It is a clinical condition that often needs to be treated through psychotherapy and sometimes with medication. Antidepressants have been found to be highly successful in treating certain people with clinical depression. Untreated depression presents a very serious emotional/mental illness and can even lead to suicide.

EXERCISE 6-2 Stress Signals Checklist

Are you suffering from stress? More than two or three of the following signs may be an indication that you should examine your life for sources of stress. Place a check mark next to any symptoms that apply to you.

___ shortness of breath   ___ irritability

___ fast or irregular pulse ___ hostility

___ nausea   ___ mood swings

___ insomnia   ___ feeling overwhelmed

___ difficulty eating   ___ difficulty concentrating

___ sadness   ___ neck or back pain

___ chronic fatigue   ___ loss of sexual interest

Behavior Modification

Some people have personalities that are much more vulnerable to stress. Whereas stress-resistant individuals are often risk-takers who realize that life has its ups and downs, stress-vulnerable individuals are often risk-avoiders who feel that new situations threaten their self-belief, which may be fragile to start out with.

People who are in the habit of thinking in negative ways about themselves are often unable to cope with change. Because of their negative thought patterns, they find many events stressful and blow little things out of proportion. Some typical thoughts of a stress-vulnerable person are:

"I can tell she doesn't like me."

"I must get this right the first time."

"I can't do anything right."

"I'll never get another job."

"It's the worst thing that could happen."

"I'm a loser."

"It's a disaster."

"It's a catastrophe."

"It's the end of the world."

With thoughts like these, it's small wonder that these people feel stressed out about their lives. If you feel like you fit into that category of individual, look back to the Route 2 chapter for some reminders on positive self-talk and "stop thought" techniques you can use.

COPING WITH STRESS

If you find yourself in a high-stress period, as in the case of being fired or splitting up with your spouse, try to head off stress at the pass as much as you can. When stress is allowed to build up, it seems to do so by leaps and bounds for a "snowball effect" where the stress quickly threatens to be overwhelming.

There are three ways you can cope with stress (**coping mechanisms**): by identifying and dealing with the cause of the stress; by changing the way you think about what's causing your stress; or by relieving the physical and emotional symptoms of stress. You can use a combination of these approaches to manage stress. In addition, you would do well to learn how to enlist the support of family and friends to help you through periods of high stress. That's what they're there for...or at least that's what they *should* be there for.

Dealing with the Cause

As much as you can, it is wise to identify the cause of your stress and deal with it decisively, either to lessen it or get rid of it altogether. For instance, suppose you have a high-stress job, like being a cab driver in New York City. You might decide to go for a less stressful job outside of New York City, if the situation of your life would permit such a change. Perhaps you would become a delivery driver with a regular route back and forth to the airport.

Let's say you have a job at a high-powered, fast-track salon and you're making good money but you're working too hard and too long seven days a week. You might decide to go for a less glamorous job in your field, with less income-earning potential, but more time for yourself.

You should also be aware not to pile up too many stress points in too concentrated an amount of time. So if you're starting a new job, that may not be the best time to buy a puppy, go on the grapefruit diet, have cosmetic surgery, and take out a home equity loan to redo your kitchen.

Reframing Your Thoughts

Perhaps the most effective way to deal with stress is by radically altering the way you think about a stressful situation (Figure 6-1). This kind of radical altering is known as **reframing**. In reframing, you can change the meaning of an event. Being fired from a job, although stressful, can also be seen as an avenue out of a rut and into something more exciting and long-lasting. A divorce is stressful, but it can also be seen as the sad ending of a troubled situation and the beginning of new opportunity for personal fulfillment. In a stressful situation that is not quite so far-reaching, such as giving a speech, you can reframe your thoughts by redirecting them away from your anxiety to focus with renewed energy on your preparation and rehearsing. In this way, you acknowledge your anxiety without letting it rule you.

Relieving the Symptoms of Stress

We've spoken about the toll that stress can take on one's health, and so it is important to get that stress under control. It would be excellent to be able to use some of the coping mechanisms mentioned above—dealing with the cause and reframing your thoughts—but sometimes, as in the case of a death in the family or the trauma of your own physical illnesses, to cite two examples, your stress might not respond to these techniques. And so the stress is with you but you

Negative Thought Pattern **Positive Thought Pattern**

FIGURE 6-1 Stress can be managed by reframing your perception of an event.

cannot afford to let it get the better of you. This is the time to pull out your arsenal of anti-stress weapons:

- **Rest and leisure.** Your body and mind are working very hard, even overtime, in a stressful period. You must insure that they get some time off, and the way to do this is with adequate rest and the conscious pursuit of leisure activities that relax you. A good night's sleep, if possible; a nap, if possible; an hour spent gardening or knitting or changing the oil in your car...whatever works for you. That's time out from stress, and you not only deserve it, but you badly need it.

- **Aerobic exercise.** There is no better medicine than an hour or 30 minutes devoted to jogging, walking, swimming, stepping, danceaerobics or any other regular aerobic exercise that will help you work off that tension. Try it...you'll like it!

- **Relaxation techniques.** You might want to explore deep breathing, yoga, meditation or other techniques that help relax and restore your body and mind. Ask around for local practitioners or, if none are available, you can try learning these techniques from books and videos.

- **Diet.** It is extremely important when you're in a high-stress period to eat the right foods. Grains, fruits, and vegetables (eaten without protein) will help calm your mood. Certain herbal teas and infusions, such as chamomile, catnip, hops, and rose hips, have been found to be beneficial. Make sure to avoid foods that create stress on your system, like colas, caffeine, fried foods, junk foods, sugar, white flour products, and chips.

- **Stress-relieving drugs.** If your stress continues despite all of the above, speak with your physician, who may want to prescribe a stress-relieving drug for you. Although tranquilizers can be effective in reducing anxiety, they do not reduce the *causes* of anxiety, so it is important not to become solely reliant on them. The most well-known tranquilizer is diazepam (sold under the brand name Valium). It is a depressant which slows down activity in the central nervous system and has the effect of calming people down. The side effects of diazepam include drowsiness (the use of this drug can interfere with driving and the operation of machinery) and may affect a person's long-term memory. Thus, taking diazepam while studying is not a good idea. Also, diazepam must never be taken in combination with alcohol; this can lead to coma or even death.

- **Seeking social support.** In looking for ways to deal with stress, don't ignore the resources of family and friends, who may be able to help you figure out and resolve the causes of your stress. For example, if you are overwhelmed by the balancing act of work and family, a helpful relative (mother, father, aunt, uncle, sister, brother) might be available to take on a few responsibilities, like chauffeuring a child around or doing some shopping for you. They might be able to provide you with useful information or just an ear. Friends, of course, are invaluable resources when you're trying to deal with stress. Just calling up a buddy for a walk or a movie can be exactly the "medicine" you need in any given moment.

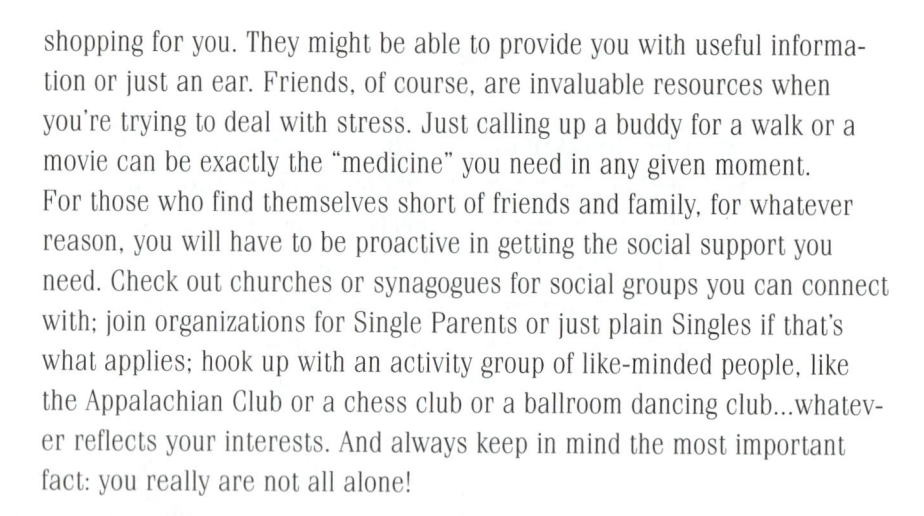

For those who find themselves short of friends and family, for whatever reason, you will have to be proactive in getting the social support you need. Check out churches or synagogues for social groups you can connect with; join organizations for Single Parents or just plain Singles if that's what applies; hook up with an activity group of like-minded people, like the Appalachian Club or a chess club or a ballroom dancing club...whatever reflects your interests. And always keep in mind the most important fact: you really are not all alone!

Reaching Out into the World

Once you've started to get a handle on your stress, you can begin to examine and improve the way you relate to other people. Keep in mind that for all people, this issue of how to improve our interrelationships is ongoing. No one is an absolute genius at getting along with others. We all have things to learn...and to remember. But let's start with you.

What kind of person are you? How do others see you? Are you a person who looks to achieve rapport with other people? To do so, you have to respect other people and trust them. You have to possess a degree of empathy, so that you can experience another person's feelings or ideas as if they were your own. You should avoid "SAD" comments—Sarcastic, Accusing, or Demeaning remarks that break down any chance of rapport.

Operating with trust, respect, and empathy does not turn you into a pushover, by any means. You can be all of those things—trustful, respectful, and empathetic—at the same time that you have a healthy **assertiveness**. Assertiveness shows that you understand the importance of your own feelings and rights just as well as you do the next person's. For instance, let's say that you're a member of a sorority and you've been asked to head up the committee that is organizing a Walk-a-Thon to raise money for juvenile diabetes. It's a good cause but there's absolutely no way you can handle this job right now. You're stretched beyond your limits as it is, with your school and family commitments, and if you accept this, it's going to be impossible. If you are a passive sort of personality, you will agree to head up the committee. You will eventually resent it and become sullen and perhaps you will wind up not doing such a good job out of spite. If you are an aggressive personality, you will chew out whoever has hit you up for this thankless job, and you will create an enemy for yourself. If you are assertive, however, you will explain why you cannot do this job right now and your refusal will be framed firmly yet politely. No hurt feelings...no harm done.

A Little Assertive Training, Anyone?

So how do you learn to become assertive? (Always keep in mind that assertive does not mean aggressive.) It's like anything else: there's a right way and a wrong way to do it. We're interested in cluing you in to the right way, so that you'll be able to say "no" to people or disagree with them and still be polite and well thought of.

The first thing you should learn to do is to frame your response as a three-part communication using these key phrases: (1) I feel..., (2) I want..., and (3) I will....

Here is an example: "I *feel* that it would be a mistake for me to take on more responsibility right now, when I'm so stretched, so I'm going to decline the job of heading up the Walk-a-Thon Committee. However, I *want* to support it, even though I don't have any real time to spare. How about if I take on a smaller job? I *will* put up posters if you give me a few dozen."

Notice that this kind of response focuses on the speaker's thoughts and feelings but also shows trust, empathy, and respect. It strikes an equal balance between the speaker's feelings and the receiver's needs.

Assertiveness is a skill that must be practiced in order for you to get better at it. Some people are just naturally good at it; others have a lot to learn. Many companies today find that assertiveness is such an important interpersonal skill that they offer employees training in assertiveness techniques. There are also many books out on this subject. You will find assertiveness techniques useful in your personal relationships as well as your work relationships. Being able to state your needs and wishes without sounding aggressive, resentful, sullen or whiney, is a tool of enormous importance as you make your way in the world.

EXERCISE 6-3 The Fine Line Between Assertiveness and Aggression

Think for a moment about a situation in which you reacted passively and found yourself doing something you really didn't want to do, or in which you reacted aggressively and found yourself involved in an argument.

1. What was the situation?
   _____
   _____

2. How did you react?
   _____
   _____

3. What do you think you could have done to protect your rights and feelings without harming the other person?
   _____
   _____

4. Reframe your response using the "I feel..., I want..., I will..." model.
   _____
   _____

HOW DO YOU RELATE TO OTHERS?

Becoming assertive in a healthy way will help you immeasurably in your dealings with people, but, in order to be really successful in our relationships, we have to come back to the issue of how we see other people. People often have difficulty relating to and communicating with people of other races, ethnic backgrounds, age groups or even genders. (Think of the book *Men Are From Mars, Women Are From Venus!*). To overcome these barriers, it is important to be open to different ways of being. It is also important to keep in mind that, whatever the differences are between people, all people still have much in common. There are basic needs, hopes, fears, and emotions that we all share. Understanding these human feelings and empathizing with others forms the basis for good relationships with people.

Most people, when they first meet someone, tend to be somewhat cautious and guarded about revealing themselves. As you reveal more about yourself to another person, a certain degree of trust and empathy develops. The other person also begins to let down his or her guard and gradually the relationship becomes deeper and more intimate. The quality of a relationship depends on the degree of mutual trust and openness that is achieved.

THE JOHARI WINDOW

One way to diagram the effect of mutual understanding and knowledge on a relationship is to use the **Johari window** (Figure 6-2). The Johari window is named after its inventors, Joseph Luft and Harry Ingham. It is a square with four sections, each section representing information known or unknown to yourself and others.

The Known. The first section of the Johari window is characterized by openness, shared information, and mutual understanding. The more intimate and productive the relationship becomes, the larger this section of the window grows. If you sketched a Johari window representing your relationship with a lifelong friend, this section would be much larger than the others. On the other hand, it might be quite small if you sketched your relationship with your new boss. If you are a shy individual, this section might remain small across the board.

The Blind Spot. The second section of the Johari window consists of feelings, behaviors, and information that is known to the other person but not to you. This blind spot in a new acquaintance might consist of information about him or her (he/she is gay, adopted, has had cosmetic surgery, used to be a nun...whatever) or about his or her perceptions of you (he/she finds you irresistible, unattractive, annoying). Whatever is unknown to you in a relationship is a handicap. Therefore, the larger this section, the less effective you are in the relationship.

	Known to self	Unknown to self
Known to others	1 The known	2 The blind spot
Unknown to others	3 The mask	4 The unknown

FIGURE 6-2 The Johari window diagrams the amount of shared and unshared knowledge in a relationship.

The Mask. This third section of the window consists of the material that you are keeping private from other people. It is your protective mask. Let's say you are gay or diabetic or take antidepressants or are a recovering alcoholic. You may want to keep any or all of these aspects hidden under your mask. It gives you a sense of power to be in control of this information. But if the mask becomes so large that it crowds out the known part of the Johari window, then the relationship will suffer and perhaps even die from lack of trust and rapport.

The Unknown. The fourth section of the Johari window consists of matters that are unknown to both people. These matters include information about the context of the relationship, each person's psychological makeup, personality traits, creative potential, and so on. As a relationship develops, the size of this section of the Johari window may decrease (Luft, 1984).

As you have probably realized, the four sections of the Johari window are not fixed in size. As a relationship develops and changes, so the sections change. By being open, trusting, and sharing information, you can decrease the size of your mask and increase the size of the known. Doing this is not always easy, especially for shy people or for people who have aspects to them that may unfortunately carry some societal stigma (e.g. sexual orientation, physical handicap, etc.) The more you can increase the known, however, the more likely you are to be able to enjoy a fruitful relationship with other people, and the more fruitful relationships you have, the more you can enjoy the world, prosper from your connections, and develop a supportive community.

FEEDBACK IN RELATIONSHIPS

Former Mayor Ed Koch of New York City used to be known for asking anyone and everyone, "How'm I doin'?" Everybody needs to know how they're doing and finding yourself in the position of either giving or receiving **feedback** in a relationship can be fraught with tension and insecurity. But it doesn't have to be!

Receiving Feedback

As a student, you will probably find yourself quite often in the position of receiving feedback, whether it be in the form of grades, written assessments, or teacher conferences. Receiving positive feedback presents no problem, but receiving negative feedback can be tough. Even though on one level, we know we are not perfect, it's one thing knowing it and another thing having it told to us. Our first reaction is often a defensive one. Rather than being open to criticism, we react by protecting our self-belief. This self-belief is so important to us that we've developed a whole system of ways to protect it made up of what is called

defense mechanisms. Among the most common defense mechanisms are withdrawal, rationalization, substitution, fantasy, and projection. Let's look at how each one works:

1. *Withdrawal.* Let's say our teacher tells us something we don't want to hear—that we are, for instance, disorganized. The first defense mechanism that comes to the fore might be *withdrawal*. We attempt to deal with the anxiety created by the negative feedback by withdrawing, or trying to avoid the stress situation altogether. Maybe we cut class for the next few days, so we can stay home and lick our wounds.

2. *Rationalization.* Another way to defend your self-belief is rationalization, which means to explain or excuse an unacceptable situation in terms that make it acceptable to yourself. Rationalizing is essentially bending the truth to make it less painful. So when your teacher tells you that you are disorganized, you might rationalize by saying (either out loud or to yourself) that you really aren't, it's just that your roommate is such a slob that everything gets messed up.

3. *Displacement.* With this defense mechanism, a person reacts to a negative situation by substituting another person for the person who aroused your anger or anxiety. To go back to our example, you are angry at your teacher for telling you that you're disorganized so you go home and pick a fight with your little sister to get rid of some of that anger. Or maybe you kick your dog?

4. *Fantasy.* With this defense mechanism, you take a road out of reality into daydreams that represent something far more pleasant. Instead of being disorganized, you are suddenly Ms. Organization...as well as Miss Congeniality and Miss America. Oh, aren't you something!

5. *Projection.* With the widely-used defense mechanism of **projection**, you attribute your own shortcomings to another person. Your teacher tells you that you're disorganized. Well, what about him? What about that time he was late? And did you ever notice how he buttons his cardigan sweater wrong?

All of these defense mechanisms serve some purpose in that they hold our heads together and help us maintain our sometimes shaky self-belief. But they come with a price. People who are always using defense mechanisms—that is, defensive people—find it hard to change and grow. Their relationships with others are marked by a lack of openness and trust.

So how can you handle negative feedback in a positive way? By paying careful attention to what's actually being said, rather than how you're feeling about what's being said. Try these tips:

- Pay attention to who is criticizing you. Is the person in a position to know what he or she is talking about? If not, then the criticism may not be valid. If so, listen up.

- Is it possible that the person who is criticizing you might actually be upset about something else? Is he or she stressed out? Do you happen to know that he or she had a baby three weeks ago, is sleep-deprived, and may simply be venting?

- Ask for specific information. Many people who offer criticism do so in the most general terms, which is not helpful. Remember to ask as well for specific measures that you can use to improve.

- Think about what you've heard. Let it sink in. Give yourself some appropriate reaction time.

- Rationally come to the decision as to whether the criticism is well-taken or not. If it is, think about what you will do to change your behavior. Canvass the opinions of friends and family to get their input on the criticism. Maybe they've been wanting to tell you the same thing too for a long time, and maybe it's time for you to hear it.

Giving Feedback

Right now you may not be so much in the position of giving people feedback professionally, but one day you may well be and, what's more, you are surely giving people feedback in other contexts. You may be giving your boyfriend feedback on how he's holding up his end of the relationship, or you may be providing feedback to your son or daughter on his or her school performance. Again, giving positive feedback is usually a pleasure all around, but giving negative feedback can be just as hard for the giver as the receiver.

If you find yourself in the position of having to give someone negative feedback, keep in mind that the person being helped must always feel respected and valued, not demeaned. Be calm, concerned, and encouraging when offering feedback and direct your comments toward behavior, not personality. When you offer feedback in a relationship, keep these things in mind:

- Understand your own feelings and motivations.

- Be accepting and nonjudgmental about the other person.

- Be sensitive to the other person's resistance. Pressure doesn't work in the long run.

- Criticize specific behavior, not personality.

- Give feedback only on matters that the other person can change. If something cannot be changed, there's little value in bringing it up.
- Don't tell others what to do.

Conflict

Even with the best intentions and a real sense of the dynamics between people, any relationship has the potential of erupting into conflict at some time or another. In fact, there's a saying that people aren't really in love until they've had their first fight.

What causes conflicts? Just about anything. Differences over ideas, facts, goals, needs, attitudes, beliefs, and personalities all cause conflict. Some conflicts are easily resolved. If you maintain, for instance, that Roger Bannister was the first man to break the five-minute mile and your friend says it was Peter Snell, you can end your disagreement by simply going to an almanac, checking it out, and finding that the right answer was Roger Bannister. You win, and, if you don't gloat obnoxiously, that should be the end of the conflict right then and there.

Conflicts about ideas, beliefs, personalities, and values, however, can be much more serious and far-reaching and can lead to frustration and anger. Unless the anger is dealt with properly, the conflict cannot be resolved.

The issue of how you handle anger also gets very complicated, because different people handle anger in different ways, and each way comes with its own set of complications.

Expressing Anger Directly. A direct expression of anger can be very aggressive. Someone cuts in line in front of you at the movies and you yell at them. Someone cuts in front of you driving and you start a road-rage duel. Obviously, these aggressive displays do not help anyone and can sometimes lead to tragic results. People with negative self-belief often have an underlying attitude of hostility that is easily triggered even by minor events and they tend to vent that hostility inappropriately. Anger can be expressed directly, however, in a way that is *assertive* rather than *aggressive*, as we talked about earlier in this chapter. Assertive expressions of anger can serve to clear the air and can be a very effective way of resolving conflict.

Expressing Anger Indirectly. Sometimes you simply don't have the luxury to express your anger directly, even if you have a whopping good reason to be angry. Let's say you're working at a salon and a regular customer chews you out for keeping her waiting five minutes. She's acting like a jerk, of course, but your job could be jeopardized if you express your anger directly. Instead, you may find yourself displacing it. Perhaps you vent onto the next person who comes into your line of vision—the poor fellow who sweeps off the floor. Now who's the jerk?

Internalizing Anger. Some people make a habit—a bad habit—of keeping all their anger bottled up inside of them. Perhaps they were raised to believe that displays of anger were rude, crude, threatening, or bad. So instead of expressing their anger, they internalize it and thus brew a simmering resentment. With no expression of anger, there is no opportunity to resolve the conflict and this festering, internalized anger can cause stress and harm to your physical and emotional well-being.

Controlling Your Anger

Fortunately, there are some useful ways to modify your behavior and control that anger that may be shaping up as a destructive force in your life. Keep the following in mind:

- Don't say or do anything immediately. The old advice to count to ten is sage advice indeed. It allows you the time to cool off and give yourself a chance to do some rational thinking.

- Figure out what it is you're so angry about. Maybe the buttons that are being pushed have more to do with the past (a parent who habitually belittled you, let's say) than the present (a teacher who is recommending that you be more organized).

- Channel your anger into physical exercise. A good long walk...a run...some time with a punching bag. All of it helps.

- Use relaxation techniques such as deep breathing to calm yourself.

Resolving Conflicts

Conflicts that go unresolved for too long become that much harder to ever resolve. Once your anger is under control, take charge of the situation and see if you can't resolve the conflict that caused it. The energy unleashed by your anger can be channeled into the problem-solving. Here are a few suggestions:

- Commit yourself to resolving the problem that caused the conflict. It *can* be done! Don't give up on it.

- Ask yourself what you're looking for in terms of a resolution. Will you only accept an apology? Is it critical for you to get your way? Your objective will influence how the conflict plays itself out.

- Make sure you and the other person have the same understanding of what the conflict is about. Ask questions and listen hard. You may be surprised—some conflicts are the result of simple misunderstandings and mixed messages.

- Be assertive, not aggressive. Remember that the other person has rights, feelings, and a point of view, too.

- Try to keep to the facts. Deal in the present. Don't bring up an entire history of transgressions. And make sure you can separate out the facts from the feelings.

At first, you may find it difficult to control your anger and have a productive conflict resolution, but, with practice and guidance you will surely get better at it. Hopefully, you will discover that by effectively resolving conflicts, you can learn more about yourself and you can grow. You'll also be able to improve the quality of your relationships with the people around you. And that's what it's all about, isn't it?

REFERENCES

Holmes, T. H. & Rahe, R. H. (1967). The social readjustment rating scale. *Journal of Psychosomatic Research*, 11, 213-218.

Luft, J. (1984, 1970, 1969). *Group processes: An introduction to group dynamics.* With permission by Mayfield Publishing, Mountain View, CA.

Masuda, M. (1974). Life changes and illness susceptibility. In B. S. Dohrenwend & B. P. Dohrenwend (Eds.), *Stressful life events: Their nature and effects.* New York: Wiley.

ROUTE SEVEN

WHERE DID THE TIME GO? STAYING ON TOP OF YOUR SCHEDULE

KEY TERMS

procrastination
setting priorities
scheduling
flexibility
simplicity

Do you know anybody these days who isn't complaining about being time-poor? Dual-career couples are barely able to keep their heads above water. Children are stretched thin between school, sports activities, or music lessons. Even retirees feel stressed out as they overschedule their golf, bridge, yoga lessons, power walking, meditation, and mah-jong.

Nothing symbolizes the tyranny of time that has overtaken our culture quite so well as the digital clock and watch. In the old days, we had the circular analog dial, whose hands rotated in what was perceived as blocks of time, let's say fifteen minutes at a sweep. Now, with digital displays, every second and every minute counts as we watch those minutes and seconds slipping away. But the question we have to ask ourselves is whether those minutes really are slipping away. Are things on the time front really as bad as we think they are?

Here's a simple test for you to try with a friend who has a digital watch that measures out time in seconds. Sit back, relax, and close your eyes. Then, when your friend says, "Go," see if you can sense how long it takes for a minute to pass. Most people will think that the minute is up when only thirty seconds have passed. Funny how time slips away, isn't it?

Naturally, when minutes seem to last only thirty seconds long, it's inevitable to feel that we're losing precious time. It's a feeling that scratches up an even deeper feeling—that somehow we're not in control of our lives—and this feeling can create a great deal of stress in an individual. But while we may not be able to control the *passage* of time, at least we can take some comfort in knowing that, with reeducation and practice, we can learn to control our *use* of time. With the help of certain basic time-management techniques, we can overcome natural human tendencies like procrastination and time-wasting. We can do our best to make the most of the limited time we have by planning and setting priorities.

Keeping a time log can also prove a revelation when it comes to figuring out where the time goes. You'll also need to learn how to use a planner and how to keep "to do" lists. By the time we're through, you're going to have a handle on the subject of time, along with some good habits that will help you find extra time where and when you need it.

HAVE YOU GOT THE TIME?

Some of us have a really hard time dealing with time. We put things off; we're chronically late; we complain about never having enough time while wasting that precious time. We never feel like we're catching up; it's almost as if we're running a race with no finish line in sight. But time *can* be managed wisely, if you know what you're doing. The first business at hand, however, is to identify the nature of your problem.

Procrastination

Procrastination is the fine art of putting off until tomorrow what you can and should do today. Scarlett O'Hara is perhaps literature's most famous procrastinator—she was always telling herself "to think of it tomorrow...at Tara." Some people are such dyed-in-the-wool procrastinators that they use up large chunks of precious time just figuring out ways to put off what has to be done!

What leads people to procrastinate? Usually, it's connected to some negative self-belief. They don't feel very competent at something, they're afraid they're going to fail, and so they put off their tasks. Other people are so dependent on outside input that they wait for starting signals, whether it be prodding from other people, the right astrological or numerological or biorhythmical moment, or the threat of something really dire happening, like failing a class or being evicted.

Some particularly deluded individuals actually fool themselves into thinking that their decision to perform a task is the same as doing the task. So if they tell themselves that they're going to complete their term paper that night, they might go off to a movie and out to dinner with the warm glowing feeling that they've overcome their problem; however, that problem is waiting for them when they come home in a timeframe that doesn't permit the assignment to be finished…or at least to be finished well.

Can procrastination be cured? The good news is yes, if you're motivated enough. Here's what you have to do (and don't fool yourself into thinking you don't have to do anything!):

- **Set a deadline for starting.** In writing, if you please. Develop a start-to-finish schedule, specifying when you will initiate a project and when you will complete it. Look at it often, so that the reality sinks in.

- **Get yourself going by starting with something easy.** If you're dreading the task—let's say getting your taxes together—start with something bearable. Sharpening pencils…sorting out a box of receipts…getting your W-2s together…you get the idea.

- **Reward yourself for progress.** If the task is large, reward yourself when you accomplish some aspect of it. A gold star, if you like that sort of thing. A new pair of shoes, if that works better for you. Dinner out. A soak in the tub. Your call, just remember to save the biggest reward for when the job is finished.

EXERCISE 7-1 Do You Procrastinate?

Many of us procrastinate, but not necessarily in all areas of our lives. Some of us keep up with our personal agenda and social relationships, while falling down on the school and/or work fronts. Others do exactly the opposite. What kind of procrastinator are you? (Be honest now.) Use the following checklist to see which areas you tend to procrastinate in.

School

___ Going to class

___ Doing homework

___ Keeping up with reading

___ Preparing papers or projects

___ Completing degree requirements

___ Studying for exams

Work

___ Arriving on time

___ Planning a career

___ Meeting deadlines

___ Looking for a job

___ Making phone calls or appointments

___ Solving a problem

Personal

___ Eating a proper diet

___ Stopping smoking or drug use

___ Pursuing hobbies

___ Exercising

___ Getting medical/dental checkups

___ Setting goals

___ Doing community service

Social

___ Visiting relatives

___ Visiting friends

___ Ending a relationship

___ Giving gifts or cards

___ Asking for a date

___ Returning phone calls

Household and Finances

___ Daily chores

___ Minor repairs

___ Paying bills

___ Balancing a checkbook

___ Car maintenance

___ Major repairs

___ Budgeting

___ Paying back loans

"Lack" of Time

Many people maintain that they don't procrastinate; they simply don't have enough time in their schedules to get everything done. They are involved in a balancing act of family, school, work, civic, and household responsibilities. Their spouses, children, parents, lovers, bosses, teachers, friends, and neighbors make constant demands on their time. They're so time-poor they haven't even been able to get their hair cut and it's a month overdue!

Yes, it's true that most of us have a great many demands on our time, but it's also true that we're lucky enough to have available to us a lot of time that wasn't there for our ancestors. We don't have to wash our laundry on a washing board and wring it out in a wringer and hang it up to dry. We don't have to kill and pluck our own chickens and few of us are into butter churning these days. So where does all that time go to?

All of us have the same number of hours in a week: 168. It's how we use those hours that is the determining factor in what gets done and what doesn't. Sometimes, when you read about people like publishing executive Michael Korda, who holds down a demanding, full-time, high-level executive position with Simon & Schuster and writes best sellers in his spare time *and* has a personal life, you think he must be super-human. But he just may be a lot more efficient at using those 168 hours a week than we are. The good news is that we can all learn to get better at using our time.

EXERCISE 7-2 How Do You Use Your Time?

If you were to keep track of your activities, you might well be surprised to find out what you actually spend your time doing. Use the time log on the following pages to record what you do over the course of a week. Include all activities, even commuting, errands, and "doing nothing," and you'll find out some surprising things about that "disappearing" time.

TIME LOG

TIME	MONDAY	TUESDAY	WEDNESDAY
7 A.M.			
8			
9			
10			
11			
12 NOON			
1			
2			
3			
4			
5			
6			
7			
8			
9			
10			
11			
12 MIDNIGHT			
1 A.M.			
2			
3			
4			
5			
6			

TIME LOG (Continued)

TIME	THURSDAY	FRIDAY	SATURDAY	SUNDAY
7 A.M.				
8				
9				
10				
11				
12 NOON				
1				
2				
3				
4				
5				
6				
7				
8				
9				
10				
11				
12 MIDNIGHT				
1 A.M.				
2				
3				
4				
5				
6				

Wasted Time and Misused Time

So you say you have no "extra" time in your busy schedule. Look at the log you filled out and see how much time you spent over dinner. The dinner "hour" stretched out to an hour and a half. You say you're a slow eater and that it's good for your digestion. But the truth is you ate your dinner in an hour and then you sat around the table for half an hour more talking with your brother about the NBA playoffs.

Okay, it's fun to talk to your brother about the playoffs and it's a nice bonding activity, but ten minutes would have done the trick, wouldn't it? Let's face it: you dawdled, you wasted time, and now it's back to the catch-up game. And you're never going to make it into the playoffs with the catch-up game you're playing.

A kissin' cousin to the issue of wasted time is misused time. Are you the sort who can turn what should be a 20-minute run to the supermarket into 40 minutes? Instead of writing down your grocery list, do you keep it in your head and get to the car and remember when you're halfway out of the lot that you forgot to buy dog food? You're spending too much time on unimportant matters, aren't you? And, consequently, your days are being eaten up by the trivial, with never enough time left over for your significant work tasks and your important leisure activities.

EXERCISE 7-3 How Well Do You Use Time?

Study the time log you filled out and then answer the following questions:

1. Total the number of hours you spent on each of the following activities.

    Sleeping _____   Eating _____   Working _____

    Classes _____   Commuting _____   Studying _____

    Chores _____   Exercising/Sports _____   Doing nothing _____

    Socializing with friends/family _____   Other (specify) _____

2. How much did you spend on worthwhile activities?
    _____

3. How much time did you waste on meaningless or trivial activities?
    _____

4. Which activities do you wish you had spent more time on?
    _____

5. Which activities do you wish you had spent less time on?

   _____

6. List any activities you meant to do but never got around to during the week you kept the time log.

   _____

MANAGING YOUR TIME

If you completed the exercises in this chapter—keeping the Time Log and looking at where you spent your time—you probably discovered that a lot of valuable time just seemed to slip through your fingers. Procrastinating, not having enough time, wasting time, and misusing time can add up dramatically, and when it does so over a period of time—months and even years—the sad news is that it deadends potential. So if you want to be in control of your life and achieve the goals you set for yourself, don't delay a moment more. Take charge of your time because, with sound time management, you will find that there *is* time to get the things done that you need to get done.

Getting Organized

The first line of attack against the tyranny of time is organization. To be organized, you have to have a firm sense of your goals and you have to plan ahead so that you can realize those goals.

Do you remember the goals we talked about in the Route 2 chapter? Those long-, intermediate-, and short-term goals? Those personal, educational, professional, and community goals? Ask yourself now how many of those goals you've lost sight of in the press of your daily routine, during which you simply try to keep your head above water.

Setting goals is vital, but why bother if you can't remember what they are? Make sure you remember. Put them on a card in your wallet (laminated is nice) or on the refrigerator. Refer back to them often so that they stick in your mind and can't be shaken loose by the hectic rush and occasional chaos of your daily life.

And don't forget the planning aspect that enters in here. After all, a goal without a plan is a dream, and when you wake up from a dream, all you have is a memory. Insure against that with some concrete planning, in which you devise an orderly, systematic approach to achieving an objective.

When you plan, be sure to take the following points into consideration:

- What you have to do.
- What resources are available to you, whether they be money, people, things, or information.
- the best way is to break down the task into manageable steps.

Another crucial aspect of getting organized is **setting priorities**. Think of it as triage. If there's a disaster in your area, the health team will use triage to prioritize health care. Urgent cases get immediate care; less urgent patients get back-burnered; patients who clearly are not going to survive the catastrophe are given less attention than patients who have a chance. You're going to want to do something like that with your goals. You need to tend first to your most immediate concerns—in your case, it may be getting through this course you're investing so much time and money into. Then, if time permits, you'll tend to concerns you feel can be managed without so much attention. Perhaps you'll cut back on time with your friends. After all, they'll understand if you need to cut back, and, if they don't, you can talk about it at some later point (if they don't, maybe they're not such great friends after all). Matters that look like they may not survive through this period of your life—your championship gymnastic career, for instance—will have to be sacrificed in favor of those pursuits which seem healthy, important, and geared to the future.

Whenever you're attempting to structure priorities, you might want to use this checklist of questions that is designed to help with the process. Ask yourself:

1. What tasks must be done immediately? (For example, buying Christmas gifts when Christmas is the day after tomorrow.)
2. What tasks are important to do soon? (Getting started on that paper that's due in two weeks.)
3. What tasks can safely be delayed for a short period? (Getting your resumé reprinted. You're not going to apply for any jobs until the Christmas season has passed.)
4. What tasks can be delayed for a week, a month, or longer? (Putting your summer clothes into the storage closet. Hey, it's only six months till summer rolls around again anyway!)

EXERCISE 7-4 Setting Your Priorities

Practicing prioritizing is important, and this exercise will help you brush up your skills. Think about the most important things you want to do this week, then write down each activity below, assigning each a priority number from 1 to 4.

1. Highest priority, cannot be delayed
2. Important, should be done as soon as possible
3. Less important, can be done next week
4. Least important, can be postponed for more than a week if necessary.

_____
_____
_____
_____
_____
_____
_____

TIME-MANAGEMENT TECHNIQUES

Now that we've addressed the issues of organization and prioritizing, let's get down to some of the nitty-gritty of time-management techniques. Essentially, these techniques are used to get you going on the science of **scheduling**. Scheduling means to factor in the time needed for fixed daily activities, such as sleeping, eating, personal hygiene, work, attending class, and so on, balanced with the left over time you're allocating to the tasks you have given the highest priority rating to. In other words, scheduling is a way to see the Big Picture and to make the most of every day as it comes.

To help schedule your time, you are going to want to purchase a planner for intermediate- and long-term scheduling along with "to do" lists for daily activities.

Planners

Think of a planner as a calendar with space in which to write. Planners come in different formats. Some rather bulky ones are a page-per-day. Some are a week-at-a-glance or a month at a time. We prefer the week-at-a-glance because it is useful to have your week visually laid out for you that way. Planners come in a wide range of sizes and styles, ranging from inexpensive ones you can pick up at discount stores, office supply stores, and pharmacies to quite luxurious ones sold at finer shops.

Your planner should be your bible when it comes to your day-to-day activities. Every single significant event in your day should go into your planner. In other words, don't put your academic schedule in one notebook, your social calendar in another, and your work requirements in a third. Consolidate everything in your planner so that you are...well, consolidated!

"To Do" Lists for Daily Activities

Virtually all planners come with pads or other inserts that allow you to keep a daily "to do" list, or, if you have room on the calendar page itself, you can keep your "to do" list there. A proper "to do" list, prepared each morning or the night before, lists all the tasks you want to accomplish that day. Don't rule out activities that may seem fairly insignificant; those are the ones that often get lost in the shuffle. We're talking about things like:

- Bring the cat into the vet for yearly shots
- Pick up Mylar for Bobby's science project
- Call Aunt Ann for her birthday
- Return videos
- Read Chapter 10 of *I'm Really Going to Do This!*

As you proceed through your day, you will continually consult your planner and you can cross off accomplished tasks as you make your way through your list.

EXERCISE 7-5 Using a Planner

Practice using a planner by filling in your time commitments for the coming week using the weekly planner on the following pages. Start by entering your routine commitments and any special appointments, whether work-related, school-related, or social. Then plan study time, work time, and leisure time accordingly.

WEEKLY PLANNER

TIME	MONDAY	TUESDAY	WEDNESDAY
7 A.M.			
8			
9			
10			
11			
12 NOON			
1			
2			
3			
4			
5			
6			
7			
8			
9			
10			
11			
12 MIDNIGHT			
1 A.M.			
2			
3			
4			
5			
6			

TIME	THURSDAY	FRIDAY	SATURDAY	SUNDAY
WEEKLY PLANNER (Continued)					
7 A.M.				
8				
9				
10				
11				
12 NOON				
1				
2				
3				
4				
5				
6				
7				
8				
9				
10				
11				
12 MIDNIGHT				
1 A.M.				
2				
3				
4				
5				
6				

EXERCISE 7-6 Doing a "To Do" List

In the space below, make a "to do" list of all the tasks you need to accomplish tomorrow. Assign each one a priority number from 1 to 4 as follows:

1. Highest priority, cannot be delayed

2. Important, should be done as soon as possible

3. Less important, can be done within a few days

4. Least important, can be postponed for a week or more if necessary

_____

_____

_____

_____

_____

_____

_____

Tomorrow, as you finish each item, cross it off.

THE FLEXIBILITY FACTOR

Having a schedule in place, written down in your planner, is a desirable goal that you should be working on, but let's face it: the best-laid planner often runs afoul. In other words, things come along—unexpected things—that tend to throw schedules out of whack, if not out the window altogether.

The ability to have organization *and* flexibility is the hallmark of someone who truly knows how to manage time. Effective time managers can handle interruptions and the demands of others. They know how to say "no" when their time is already committed. And they know how to take unexpected gifts of time and run with them.

Dealing with the Demands of Others

Picture this: you've gotten your whole day planned out, you have honed your schedule, everything is in its place, when suddenly you get a call on your cell phone that your mom's car has broken down and you have to go pick her up at the garage. Now this is your mom, the woman who raised you and made endless sacrifices for you, and you can't very well leave her stranded...*can you*? So you have to start juggling things around, and, in the process, you lose some valuable time. But, hey, it's your mom, right? *Right.*

This is called life. Mothers, fathers, husbands, wives, children, lovers, and friends are the people who matter and the people who, inevitably, make demands on you. Sometimes you can be rather cunning and avoid those demands. If, for instance, you know that your brother is going to start bugging you to give him that haircut you've been promising him, and if you have a paper due tomorrow and you don't have even ten minutes to spare, you might decide to do your studying that night in the library rather than at home. After all, the world is not going to fall apart if your brother doesn't get that haircut for a few days.

Picking your stranded mother up at the garage, however, is another issue. There are certain things you cannot avoid, and when these things come along you just have to accept the fact that they're going to play havoc with your schedule. A sick child, home from school, is a perfect example. A spouse who's been told that he has to fly out of town for an emergency business meeting, leaving you to cover the homefront. A friend who's boyfriend has just announced that he's dumping her and who needs a little emergency stroking, if not in person at least on the phone.

So how do you deal with these kinds of interruptions? You factor them into your schedule. Leave what's called "response time" in your planning book. This is a cushion of time you can use to respond to the needs of other people as they come up. If you schedule in more time than you actually need to finish a task, you can always "borrow" some of that time for these inevitable interruptions.

Learning to Say No

You would think a little two-letter word wouldn't present such a huge obstacle, but for a great many people, actually saying that little two-letter word is like pulling teeth. For a mini-review on how to say no, we refer you back to the assertiveness section in Route 6 (remember that sorority sister who had to say no when asked to chair the Walk-a-Thon committee?). But we bring up the subject again here because it is essential if you are going to stay on top of any kind of schedule, that you to have the capacity to say no. When people come to you with additional responsibilities, projects, or demands that are not absolutely crucial and which would lead to some drastic overcommitment on your part, you really need to be able to use that little two-letter word. If anyone is deeply offended (assuming you've couched your refusal in inoffensive and sensitive ways), that's their problem.

Using Unexpected Gifts of Time

Every now and then, a little gift falls into your lap: some "extra" time. Maybe an appointment has been cancelled. Maybe there's a snowstorm and you can't do anything but stay home until the roads are cleared. How do you respond to these gifts? If you are an effective manager of time, you'll respond by using them to get some extra things done.

On that snowstorm day, you might not only do the studying you had planned, but you might clean up your study area so that you can be more organized still and buy some time in the future that way. You might do both of those things and have time to play a game of Chutes and Ladders with your child...a child who sometimes feels that there's never enough time to play Chutes and Ladders with Mom or Dad.

Take the gift of time, use it, and, as with any gift, don't forget to say "thank you."

SIMPLICITY

You may have noticed in the last few years that a lot has been written in magazines and books about the idea of **simplicity**. What is meant by that? Simplicity is a way of looking at life with the idea that "less is more." You may be spending a lot of time on things that are, on reflection, unworthy of your time. Let's look at a specific situation to see how this "time-wasting" works.

It's Christmas. So much to do. Buying gifts, cooking, baking, cleaning, sending cards. But that's what Christmas is all about, right?

Wrong.

Believe it or not, Christmas was never meant to be about exhausting yourself and striving for a kind of perfection that only Martha Stewart can achieve. Christmas was meant to be about having quality time with your family and people you care about, and maybe even experiencing a few precious moments when you can actually connect to the spirituality of the holiday.

Let's think of some ways to get out of the crazy Christmas trap:

1. You're dreading the experience of making a big holiday dinner for a lot of relatives who never seem that pleased about what you do anyway. This year, what about proposing to your family that you spend Christmas working at a shelter? True, it's work, but it doesn't involve weeks of planning and preparation, and you may even find that you may experience a whole other kind of "Christmas miracle" you never would have had before.

2. You just don't feel like dealing with Christmas cards this year. Send an email around to all your friends explaining that you're not up to it, explain that you'd just as soon save a few trees, and tell them all how much you love them and wish them a joyous holiday.

3. If you are making a holiday dinner, allow yourself some shortcuts. Use a disposable roasting pan for that turkey, roast beef, or ham. It may not be ecologically sound, but once a year you can get away with it. For dessert, skip the homemade Yule log and buy some cookies and clementines. It's the company that matters anyway.

4. If you're sick of the whole process of getting out the Christmas decorations, try decorating your tree this year only with things from nature. Pine cones, bird nests, bittersweet. It's all free and you'll be amazed at how beautiful it is.

5. Don't make yourself crazy about Christmas presents. Tell yourself you're buying everyone books this year...and do it over the Internet!

The point of the above is not just about Christmas...or Easter...or Passover or whatever you choose to celebrate. It's about getting yourself into a mindset where you can figure out what *you* need to do to feel fulfilled and satisfied, rather than marching to the orders of what *others* expect of you. It's about distilling experience down to something much simpler, easier, and, ultimately, more meaningful. This is a way to find time that really works.

TIME SAVERS

The kind of simplicity described above can inspire you to start thinking about the many ways you can achieve that simplicity elsewhere in your life. Time-saving tricks are everywhere, waiting to be discovered. Here are some of our favorites:

Cooking

- Keep your shopping list on the fridge and note what you need to buy as you go through your supplies. When you go to the store, bring the list along with a friend or family member. Rip the list in half, and, between the two of you, get the job done in half the time. Also try to shop in the same store every week, so you are familiar with the aisles and where things are located.

- Develop a repertoire of good meals you can cook in thirty minutes or less. There are all kinds of excellent cookbooks out there on good, fast cooking.

- If you double the quantities as you prepare meals with the idea of freezing away the extras, you'll have two or three meals for the "time price" of one.

Around the House

- Buy several pairs of scissors and rolls of tape and place them in strategic areas around the house: kitchen, bedroom, playroom. That way you won't have to spend time looking for these things.

- Hang a hook in your kitchen or garage for house and car keys. Encourage family members to place their keys there, as you do. That way less time is chewed up searching for your keys (the same goes for your wallet—always keep it in the same place so you don't have to spend time looking for it).

- Prioritize your housecleaning: think in terms of what needs to be done on a daily basis (picking clothes up from the floor); what needs to be done every week (throwing out garbage and recyclables, probably some vacuuming); what needs to be done every month (changing your sheets...preferably more often, but certainly not longer than a month!); and what needs to be done once or twice a year (dusting the chandelier). Doing this allows you to focus on get the job done instead of spending your time inefficiently.

- If you live in a multi-story home, keep a vacuum on each level, if you can afford to do so. It saves much time and energy.

Laundry

- If you have kids, buy them white socks only. They won't care; the socks will be interchangeable; and you'll cut back drastically on time spent laundry sorting.

- A sleeping bag makes a fine alternative to linens on a child's bed. They'll think it's cool; there won't be a bed to make up; and you can just toss it in the washer and dryer every week with hardly any fuss at all.

Home Repairs

- Silhouette your tools on a pegboard so you'll always know just where things go.
- Keep all your appliance manuals and warranties in one place so you don't have to go searching for them. A ringbinder on the cookbook shelf is where we like to keep ours.
- Place electric cords, Christmas tree lights, and garden hoses on reels. Untangling these sorts of things can eat up surprising amounts of time.

Travel

- If you're a frequent traveler, keep a master list of everything you need to take with you on trips: money belt, makeup, shampoo, alarm clock, pharmaceuticals. Before you begin to pack, check off the things you'll need on that particular trip.
- Find out where you can get $25 of the currency for wherever you're headed, and get it before you set out.
- Keep an extra cosmetic bag packed just for travel, all ready to go.

This 'n That

As you get into the habit of tricking time, all sorts of ideas will start to come to you. Consider these:

- Even if your gas tank is only half empty, fill it while you're out doing other errands. This will prevent a special trip when the needle drops down to "empty."
- Check out automatic services that will save you a trip to the bank, such as paying your mortgage.
- Arrange carpools for kids' activities. Why do you always need to be the one driving?
- Don't give up on entertaining friends because it's "too much work." Embrace the idea of the covered-dish supper, with everyone bringing a course.

- Get up a half-hour earlier. Make that your "private time." Read...meditate...take a bath...do whatever you need to do to carve out some tranquility before meeting your busy day.

As you get into the habit of thinking in these ways, you'll see that there's more time in a day than you thought there was. You'll begin to feel more in control of your life, more productive, and more grounded.

Hey, it's about time, isn't it?

STAYING ON TOP OF THINGS

Olivia, 30, enrolled in school and missed only three days while acquiring the 1500 clock hours. She was the mother of three children and held a job for 30 hours per week, but still she always knew what was expected of her. Early during her cosmetology program, she had the opportunity to be involved in goal setting and time management plans. She was able to balance all of her responsibilities because she prioritized them and learned to say "no" when necessary. Following graduation, her first job was as a manager of a salon with eight stylists. She continued to achieve her goals and opened her own salon within three years of graduation. Her daughter followed in her footsteps, became a successful stylist and is now a cosmetology instructor. Olivia has instilled in her daughter the necessity for goal setting and time management, as well as a love for the beauty industry.

8 ROUTE EIGHT

SHOW ME THE MONEY (AND THEN WHAT DO I DO WITH IT?)

KEY TERMS

financial pyramid
budgeting
gross income
net income
fixed vs. variable expenses

The American writer Henry David Thoreau didn't care very much about money—that's why he went to live at Walden Pond; and then there are the Trappist monks, who don't get very worked up on the subject either, but, let's face it, most of the rest of the world does. Particularly these days, when the economy is so strong and everyone wants a piece of the action. Making good money is surely one of the reasons why you've chosen cosmetology as a career. After all, you'll be acquiring a highly marketable skill in a multi-billion dollar industry, and, if you develop an entrepreneurial bent down the line, you may even wind up owning, or co-owning, your own shop...or two shops...or a chain of shops...or who knows what?

Money is exciting and with all the Loose Change, Hot Dollars, Powerball, and Lotto fever in the air, not to mention *Who Wants to Be a Millionaire?* and all its imitators, sometimes it all seems like a great big game. Sure, there are high rollers who treat money as a great big game, but for the rest of us, money is still a limited resource. In that way, it's not so dissimilar from time, which we discussed in the last chapter. Just as we all try to manage our time to get the most of it, we all have to learn how to manage our money to get the most out of that.

In this chapter, we will introduce basic concepts of money management. But, before we touch on that, it is important to discuss people's attitudes toward money. Often people feel inhibited or confused when it comes to making money. So let's start with a very basic question: What does money mean to you?

IT'S ONLY MONEY

You can never be too rich or too thin.
Money makes the world go around.
Money is the root of all evil.
I cannot afford to waste my time making money.

These are just four, money-related quotations among the thousands that exist, but they reflect people's radically different attitudes on the subject. Some people live for that green stuff; some people live off of it; and some people try to get far away from it.

However you look at it, money is a resource that carries a high emotional charge for all of us. If your parents were generous with gifts, you might have one kind of attitude about money. If your parents were tight-fisted, money means something else altogether. If you grew up rich, you have one set of values with relation to money. If you grew up poor, it's different. If charity was part of the value system instilled within you, that may still be an important factor in the money picture for you today. In short, there are many variables, but, to borrow a money term, there's only one bottom line: money is not going to go away. Whether you use dollars, pounds, francs, yen, seashells, or whatever, money is here to stay.

Few people would dispute the fact that Americans live in a culture where a great value and emphasis is placed on money. America has always been a consumer culture, and now the rest of the world is catching up. The other great 20th century economic system—communism—has collapsed, and capitalism has rushed into the void more powerfully than ever. People all over the world are questing for material goods—often ones that are "Made in America"—and studies show that the haves and the have-nots are more widely separated than ever. Twenty years ago, a chief executive officer (CEO) of an American corporation typically made 40 times what an average employee made. Today, that same CEO is making over 400 times as much as his or her typical employee. The Internet age has ushered in a whole new race of very young, fabulously rich people, whose net worths are numbered not in millions, but in *billions*. The Dow Jones climbs to all-time records and wherever one goes these days, you're hearing about people investing on-line and making bundles.

But the bottom line—to use that phrase again—is that money isn't everything. Recently, there have been stories in the media about vastly wealthy people, whose net worth is in the upper hundreds of millions of dollars, who are seeking psychotherapy because they are depressed when they compare themselves to those young Internet folks making billions. This is when we, as a culture, have to step back and ask ourselves what is going on here? The rest of the world, plagued by overpopulation and collapsed economies, is getting poorer, and rich people in our country are worrying that they aren't rich enough.

One of the things that happens when a culture reaches the level of affluence that our culture has achieved is that the possession of money and outward signs of material worth are often equated with a person's inner worth. The more money you have, the better or more "successful" you are as a person. When money defines self-belief, people become increasingly dependent on their possessions to boost their feelings of self-worth. But possessions are things, and things can never ultimately define a person.

The issue of money is closely related to the issue of goals we spoke about in The Goal Zone (Route 2). If you recall, in that chapter we discussed the importance of striking a balance in our pursuit of personal, professional, educational, and community goals. Around the issue of money, too, we have to strike that balance. How much are we willing to dedicate ourselves to making money and at what cost to our personal lives?

But let's talk about you. How do *you* feel about money? Do you see it as the thing you need to make you a better person? Or do you view money as a tool, a very powerful tool by which you can achieve your goals, whether educational, professional, or personal? Have a look at the following exercise and see if it helps you clarify some of your attitudes about money.

EXERCISE 8-1 You & Money

Are you ready to explore your attitudes about money? Circle the answer that corresponds most closely with your feelings.

- When you think of having money, you imagine it:
    1. coming from your parents
    2. belonging to your spouse or significant other
    3. belonging to you

- As a child, you spent your allowance or pocket money on:
    1. anything you wanted
    2. necessities
    3. birthday and holiday presents for your relatives

- When you were younger, you always had a hangup about math. Now that you need to make money decisions, you:
    1. figure you can't balance a checkbook, much less use your money wisely
    2. put off making money decisions because you dislike math
    3. tell yourself that math has nothing to do with your ability to handle money

- You have just $35 to spend on food and other necessities until payday, four days from now. Passing a pizza place, you:
    1. splurge on a pizza with all the toppings
    2. keep going, since you can't even afford to look in the window
    3. promise yourself to stop in after payday to buy a pizza

- You get an unexpectedly large gift of $500. You:
    1. blow it on an expensive watch and new clothes
    2. invest in bank certificates that will tie up the money for thirty months
    3. put the money in a savings account to which you have access

- You want to go back to school. You have enough money for only a quarter of the total tuition for the program. You:
    1. enroll anyway. Something will come up to pay for the other three-quarters
    2. enroll for a couple of courses even though they're likely to be your last
    3. make a plan for financing the whole program through work, grants, and loans

- You won $30,000. You desperately need a new refrigerator and TV. You:
    1. hold off until the refrigerator breaks down and TVs go on sale
    2. put all the money in the bank and do without a new refrigerator and TV
    3. buy both
- Word of your luck has spread at school. The first time your fellow students don't ask you to join them at lunch, you:
    1. feel sorry you won the money
    2. spend lunch time buying them presents
    3. ignore them and visit a financial planner during lunch

To arrive at your score, add up the numbers you circled. Check the results below.

Your Score	What It Means
8-10 points	You tend to be very emotional about money. You should be wary of making sudden money decisions.
11-17 points	You are shaky about making money decisions. Although you probably won't make major mistakes, you also won't get the most out of your money.
18-24 points	You have an objective attitude toward money and its uses. Be sure you consider all the consequences before making a money decision.

THE FINANCIAL PYRAMID

In Route 4 (The Whole You), we presented the Food Pyramid as a visual model to quickly convey your nutritional needs. Now we've got the **Financial Pyramid**: a model that is designed to help you visualize your money management concerns.

At the base of the financial pyramid are your values and goals. This is the foundation of your life. This is what it's all about for you. If your goal is security, this is where it goes. If helping others is what you value, think of it here, at your foundation. If your value is your own personal satisfaction, and enjoying life to the fullest, this is where it goes. If your goal is to retire after the age of 45, stick it here.

The next step-up holds your basic living expenses—food, shelter, clothing, transportation, and so on. Before you can go on to spend money on other things, you have to make sure that your basic living expenses are attended to. You may be lusting for a leather jacket, but that's not going to keep you warm if you don't pay your heating bill in January.

Once you've budgeted for the basics, you can climb up to the next level of the pyramid, where you'll find issues around savings, credit, and insurance. Getting complicated? A bit perhaps, but without savings, you're living from paycheck to paycheck and even if you're young, healthy, and basically only taking care of yourself, things have a way of coming up to throw you off whatever course you've designed. You might suddenly need a root canal for $450, let's say, and you've got to put away some money for emergencies like that. Of course, there are all kinds of reasons other than emergencies to justify saving money. These include building for the future—having enough money to get married or have children or buy a home or start your own business. You'll also want to save money for those purchases that you're keeping a long-term eye on: that fancy leather jacket, for instance, or a trip to Club Med. After all, life would be pretty bleak if we never allowed ourselves some extravagant goodies. Insurance is in this tier too: health insurance, perhaps dental insurance (remember that root canal we were just talking about?), automobile insurance, home insurance if you own your own home or even if you rent, and, at a certain appropriate time in your life, life insurance. (Usually, you'll pick up some of the latter if you want to make provisions for a spouse or a child who might outlive you). Keeping your credit rating healthy is also a concern here, for you'll want to be able to borrow more money as you move up the pyramid.

And, speaking of moving up the pyramid (and borrowing money), you're now on to the next level, which is home ownership. This is, of course, a big part of the American Dream (not that you necessarily have to buy into the American Dream; maybe you'll want to spend your whole life renting a little cabin and using the lion's share of your income to travel around the world). But if you do want to own your own home, you'll need to have that savings/insurance/credit plateau in good shape, with an emphasis on the credit, because chances are you'll be borrowing big-time, in the form of a mortgage.

At the top of the pyramid are the long-term investments you may need to make, which are commonly such things as saving for your children's education and saving for your retirement.

The financial pyramid (Figure 8-1) is useful in that it helps people prioritize their money resources. It points out certain important long-term financial goals that people can start thinking about even when they're young. Keep in mind, however, that the pyramid is not "set in stone" for everyone. As we've said, you might not want to own a home. In the same vein, you might have grown up in a

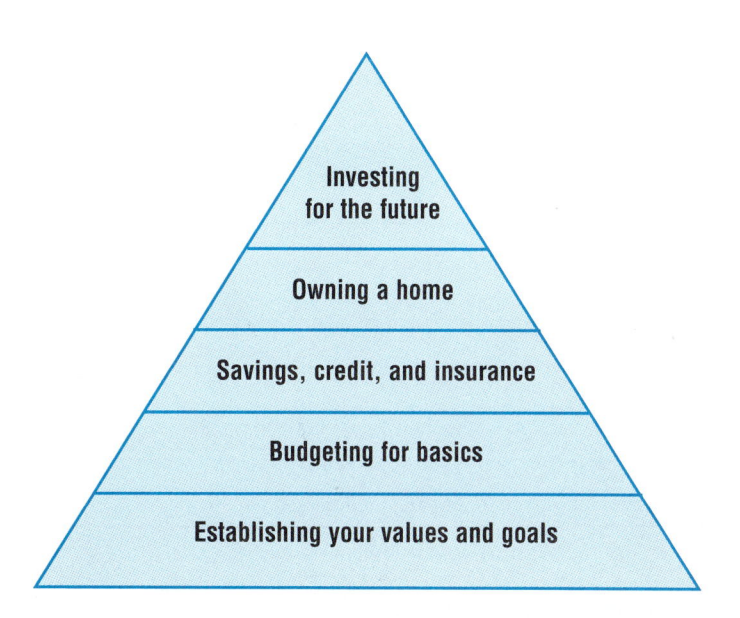

```
                    ┌─┐
                   ╱   ╲
                  ╱ Investing ╲
                 ╱ for the future ╲
                ╱─────────────────╲
               ╱   Owning a home   ╲
              ╱─────────────────────╲
             ╱ Savings, credit, and insurance ╲
            ╱─────────────────────────────────╲
           ╱      Budgeting for basics         ╲
          ╱───────────────────────────────────╲
         ╱    Establishing your values and goals ╲
        ╱─────────────────────────────────────────╲
```

FIGURE 8-1 The financial pyramid provides a basic model for financial planning.

family where credit was a dirty word and so you never carry plastic in your wallet. The order of the pyramid is one that most people experience, but its sequence is also open to variations. If you are a student living at home with your family, for instance, you may not be concerned about basic expenses—after all, your parent's house is a perfectly adequate roof over your head and Mom's always happy to share her pot roast with you—but you may have already jumped on to the next plateau, where credit resides, in the sense that you've taken out student loans.

EXERCISE 8-2 Your Goals & Money

Now is a good time to review your values and goals, as sketched out in earlier chapters. Summarize your most important values and goals below. Then underline those goals that involve money.

1. Most important goals:
   _____
   _____
   _____

2. Short-term goals:
   _____
   _____
   _____

3. Intermediate-term goals:

_____
_____
_____

4. Long-term goals:

_____
_____
_____

THE "B" WORD: BUDGETING

Oh yes, you've heard the word "budgeting" many times...but isn't that what "grown ups" do?

Well, what would you like first—the good news or the bad news? The bad news is you *are* a grown-up now. And the good news is that you're a grown-up now. So being a grown-up (which doesn't necessarily happen at age 18, age 28, or even age 38), is very much of a mixed bag. You've got the autonomy; you've got the problems; you've got it all.

And it's true that **budgeting** is something that mature people do. They have to. Budgeting means planning out how to use the money you have available to you. A budget is a plan, or a blueprint, or a guide that is based on your short-, intermediate-, and long-term financial goals. The purpose of a budget is to keep your spending within the limits of your income and to distribute your spending appropriately. Easier said than done in many cases, but definitely something to work toward.

Budgeting has many benefits. The main point of budgeting is to help you figure out where your money comes from and where it goes. But, equally important, budgeting helps you focus on your goals and encourages you to set the priorities necessary for achieving them.

Let's use an analogy. If you have a fitness plan, you may decide that you want to lose 30 pounds, gain x amount of inches around your chest and shoulders, and lose x amount of inches around your waist. To do this, you need a plan. You have to figure out how many calories a day you will take in and how many calories a day you will expend. You have to figure out how many bench presses a day is required to achieve your goal, and how much time on the track. Budgeting is like that. You know what you want to achieve—let's say you want to start your own business—so you have to figure out how much money is coming in from the two jobs you're working, how much is going out in terms of basic living expenses, loans, etc., and how much is left over for you to put into a "start your own business" fund.

Right now, starting your own business may not be in the forefront of your mind, but, even so, you probably spend a lot of time thinking about money. Chances are, you don't have enough money for all the things you want to do and all the things you think you need. We hate to be the bearer of ill tidings, but once you get a better job and your income increases, you may still be in a position of not having enough money for all the things you want to do and all the things you need. After all, as you get older, your responsibilities tend to increase. You may have children, (and they have a habit of consuming a great deal of money) or you may wind up having to take care of a parent at some point. This means that, right now, you have to start thinking about your goals and decide what is most important to you. And when it comes to budgeting, the place to begin is with your income and your expenses. In other words, what comes in and what goes out.

Income and Expenses

Maybe you're a rock star and you've got so much money coming in from record sales, concerts, foreign sales, endorsements, book sales, TV appearances and commercials that you really don't have a very clear idea altogether of how much money you have coming in...all you know is that your accountants tell you that you have enough for as many Porsche Boxsters as you'd like. If, however, you are like the rest of us, you have a reasonably good idea of where your money comes from. Your *income* is the total amount of money coming in and it may derive from any or all of the following sources:

- a salary you earn by working
- an allowance from your parents or spouse
- alimony or child support payments
- welfare payments or food stamps
- social security payments
- disability payments
- student financial aid
- tax refunds

- gifts
- interest earned on savings
- dividends earned on investments

The total amount of your income, collected from any or all of the above sources, is called your **gross income**. If you are working, your employer withholds amounts from your paycheck to pay federal and local taxes, social security (FICA), group insurance premiums, union dues, pension contributions, and other deductions. The amount of money left over is called your **net income** and, inevitably of course, it is less than your gross income.

As we've said, unless you're a rock star, you probably have a fairly firm grasp on what monies are coming in, but having a firm grasp on what monies are going out is a much harder proposition. The amount of money you spend is called your *expenses*. Most people have **fixed expenses**, which are the same from month to month or come up quarterly or yearly. These include rent money or mortgage payments, telephone and utility bills, car loan payments, insurance payments, cable TV bills and things like that. **Variable expenses** are those that come up periodically and sometimes unpredictably. Entertainment, for instance, is a variable expense in the sense that you will probably spend more money at a certain time of year—let's say New Year's Eve—than at other times of year (let's say Groundhog Day). Medical expenses are usually variable as are things like appliance and house repairs, car repairs, and things of that nature.

Now let's have a little quiz. If your expenses are higher than your income, you have a problem. True or false? If you answered True, you have a very fundamental grasp of money matters. You should always have more money coming in than going out: Basic Law of Nature, Rule # 1. This can be accomplished, in most cases, by improving your money situation through budgeting.

The Four A's of Budgeting

There are four basic steps to budgeting, which you should think of as the four A's (O'Neill & Wyss, 1991). They are:

1. accounting for income and expenses
2. analyzing your situation
3. allocating your income
4. adjusting your budget

Accounting for Income and Expenses. You won't get past the first of the four A's if you don't keep track of your income and expenses for at least a couple of months. You need to note not only big expenditures like car payments, but small ones, like renting a video or buying an ice cream cone. If you have a checking account, or if you've made most of your purchases with a credit card, you will have built-in records of your expenditures, assuming you cast an eye on your cancelled checks and credit card summaries.

An important way to track income and expenses is to maintain a notebook, set up as shown below. Divide the notebook into two sections: a small section where you record your income and a larger section where you record your expenses. Whenever you get paid or otherwise receive money, enter the date, source, and amount in the income section. Whenever you spend money—whether it be 75 cents for a newspaper, $2.95 for a mocha latte, or $42.95 for that little cotton sweater you just had to have—jot down the date, what you bought, and how much you paid for it in the expenses section. Don't forget to enter those purchases you made with a credit card—those weren't free, you know!

To make your record-keeping easier, you can organize your expenses section into such categories as Rent, Telephone, Utilities, Food, Clothing, Transportation, Medical/Dental, Entertainment, Personal Items, Gifts, Miscellaneous, and so on. At the end of each month, total your income and then total your expenses by categories. These figures will serve as the basis of what will become your budget.

EXERCISE 8-3 Track Your Income and Expenses

Use the income and expense record on the following pages to keep track of all your income and expenses for two months.

Income and Expense Record, Month of _____

Income

Date	Source	Net Amount
	Total	

Expenses

Date	Rent/Mortgage	Telephone	Utilities	Insurance	Loan	Transportation	Food
Totals							

Date	Clothing	Household	Medical	Education	Savings/Emerg.	Personal	Other
Totals							

Total expenses for month _____

Income and Expense Record, Month of _____

Income

Date	Source	Net Amount
	Total	

Expenses

Date	Rent/Mortgage	Telephone	Utilities	Insurance	Loan	Transportation	Food
Totals							

Date	Clothing	Household	Medical	Education	Savings/Emerg.	Personal	Other
Totals							

Total expenses for month _____

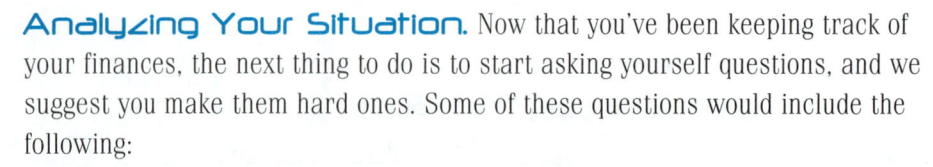

Analyzing Your Situation. Now that you've been keeping track of your finances, the next thing to do is to start asking yourself questions, and we suggest you make them hard ones. Some of these questions would include the following:

- Did your expenses exceed your income? (Ouch).
- Were you able to pay all your fixed expenses? (Ouch again).
- Did a large periodic expense such as snow tires or a tuition bill throw you off? (Please...stop!)
- Did you pay off all your credit card balances? (Are you kidding?) Did you at least pay the minimum payment? (Yes, sir. You betcha).
- Were you able to save money for one of your goals, like a new stereo or a vacation? (Yeah, right...weekend in Newark!).

Allocating Your Income. Okay, not to panic. We see that you've kept track of your income and expenses for the last few months and patterns are emerging. It's a little depressing, isn't it? You have this sinking feeling that you're never going to have enough money to reach your goals at this rate. But don't despair—there are things you can do. Lots of things!

First of all, you need to figure out how much you have to allocate to your fixed expenses each month. These fixed expenses are holy. They include the bills you pay monthly (rent, electricity, telephone, and credit card payments) and those that you pay on a quarterly, semiannual, or yearly basis that have to be factored in (insurance premiums, tuition, taxes, etc.). Let's say you noticed that you were caught short for that semiannual car insurance premium. If you had set aside a certain amount of money each month to cover that, you wouldn't have had to borrow the funds from your parents to pay that one off. To put it in dollars and cents, if the cost of your car insurance premium is $600 a year, you need to be allocating $50 each month toward that expense so you don't get caught short again.

After you've budgeted your fixed expenses, turn your attention to those variable expenses that are eating up a lot of your money. This is where you can cut back. You didn't really need that little cotton sweater, did you? (Your boyfriend actually said the color made you look green anyway). That money, close to $50, could have been the month's allotment toward your yearly car insurance premium we mentioned above. Eating out is an area that "eats up" huge amounts of money. Going out to the movies instead of renting a video is another extravagance that can be cut back on. We're not suggesting that you never go out or buy anything just for the fun of it. We're simply saying that you might not be in the position to do as much of that as you are currently doing.

Next, consider what you would do if your car broke down and you needed a $300 repair. These things happen all the time and often happen in clusters, for some reason. It's called life (remember that board game?). What you need for such events is an *emergency fund*. An emergency fund is essentially two months' income that is put away for...well, emergencies! This is not an easy thing to accomplish, but you can start amassing your emergency fund by going cold turkey on the little cotton sweaters for a while, and any cash gifts you receive from family for birthdays or Christmas could go into this fund. And don't forget—when you dip into the fund, you have to replenish it. It doesn't fill up again all by itself!

Finally, consider your goals. If you have your heart set on taking a real vacation—a week in January in Cancun, let's say—you've got to start saving for it well in advance, even if it's only a few dollars a month. And every time you see a little cotton sweater, you can tell yourself you'd rather be lying on a beach this winter anyway...where you don't need any sweaters at all!

Adjusting Your Budget. A budget is not carved in stone. As you try out your budget, maybe you'll find that you haven't planned realistically or that you've forgotten some items altogether. Your income is going to change; your expenses are going to change; your life is going to change and your goals will change accordingly. For these reasons, you need to review your budget periodically and see where it needs to be nipped and tucked.

EXERCISE 8-4 Make Up a Monthly Budget

Use the information you gathered and analyzed to allocate your income on a monthly basis. In the space below, enter the dollar amounts you plan to spend on each of the following expenses for a period of one month.

Item	Budgeted Amount
Rent/mortgage	_____
Telephone	_____
Utilities (gas, oil, electricity, water, sewer)	_____
Cable TV/Internet access	_____
Insurance (auto, health, life, homeowners', disability, etc.)	_____
Installment loans	_____
Transportation (gas, maintenance, repairs, parking, carfare)	_____
Food (groceries and restaurant meals)	_____
Clothing	_____

Item	Budgeted Amount
Household items and repairs	_____
Gifts	_____
Medical/dental	_____
Education (tuition, books, fees)	_____
Personal (including entertainment)	_____
Emergency fund	_____
Taxes not withheld (self-employment, excise, real estate)	_____
Savings toward goals	_____
Other	_____

SAVINGS AND CREDIT

Savings and Banking

These days, sticking your money under your mattress is no longer considered the norm. That's what we have banks for. Some amount of cash is usually kept on hand, and the rest of your money is kept in a bank or a financial institution, whether it be a commercial bank, savings and loan, or credit union. When selecting a financial institution in which to deposit your funds, you should consider the following:

- Up to what amount are your deposits insured and by whom. Federal insurance, such as the FDIC, is a better risk than state insurance funds, some of which have gone broke in the past.
- Interest rates.
- How accessible your money is to you.
- Convenience of location and hours.
- The types of accounts that are offered.

It's entirely possible that you'd want to distribute your money among various accounts. For instance, almost everyone needs a *checking account* to pay routine bills (Figure 8-2). You would deposit a portion of each paycheck and other earnings into this checking account and from that you would write checks to pay your bills, keeping a record of each deposit and check in the check register. Checking accounts vary a great deal from one to the other. Some pay interest if you keep a minimum balance. Some charge you for each check you write; others charge a

FIRST TRUST BANK
Central Avenue Branch
Vero Beach, FL 12312

PAGE 1 OF 1

JOHN J. BROWN
123 Elm Court
Vero Beach, FL 12345

002 613 CY

13435711
6134357116

STATEMENT OF YOUR ACCOUNT(S) FOR PERIOD 11-15-00 THROUGH 12-13-00

SUMMARY OF REGULAR ACCOUNT # 18 485711

BALANCE LAST STATEMENT	502.10
DEPOSITS AND OTHER ADDITIONS	1910.78
CHECKS AND OTHER SUBTRACTIONS	1306.12
BALANCE THIS STATEMENT	1106.76

TAXPAYER ID NUMBER 123 45 6789

DATE	TYPE OF TRANSACTION	CHECKS	SUBTRACTIONS	ADDITIONS	BALANCE
11-15	BEGINNING BALANCE				502.10
11-18	DEPOSIT			405.24	907.34
11-22	CHECKS POSTED (3)	67.20			840.14
11-23	DEPOSIT			650.15	
11-23	CHECKS POSTED (1)	17.75			1472.54
11-25	CHECKS POSTED (4)	519.45			953.09
11-28	CHECKS POSTED (1)	44.00			909.09
11-29	CHECKS POSTED (3)	47.20			861.89
11-30	DEPOSIT			305.24	
11-30	CHECKS POSTED (1)	50.00			1117.13
12-05	CHECKS POSTED (3)	363.27			753.86
12-06	CHECKS POSTED (1)	149.69			604.17
12-07	DEPOSIT			305.24	909.41
12-08	CHECKS POSTED (1)	4.00			905.41
12-09	CHECKS POSTED (1)	43.56			861.85
12-12	DEPOSIT			244.91	1106.76

CHECKS POSTED (* INDICATES SEQUENCE BREAK)

CHECK	AMOUNT	DATE	CHECK	AMOUNT	DATE	CHECK	AMOUNT	DATE
7242	50.00	11-30	7249	21.20	11-29	7255	16.00	11-29
7243	44.00	11-28	7250	6.70	11-25	7256	10.00	11-29
7244	17.75	11-23	7251	47.20	11-22	7257	13.27	12-05
7245	10.00	11-22	7252	10.00	11-22	7258	43.56	12-09
7246	400.00	11-25	7253	17.66	11-25	7259	300.00	12-05
7247	50.00	12-05	7254	93.09	11-25	7260	149.69	12-06
7248	4.00	12-08						

FIGURE 8-2 The financial pyramid provides a basic model for financial planning.

monthly fee with unlimited check-writing. It's best to shop around to find the most advantageous checking account to suit your needs.

Large sums of money, if you should be so lucky as to have some, are not designed to be kept in checking accounts, which pay little or no interest. Instead, you'll want to put extra money into a savings account that pays compound interest. With compound interest, you get interest both on the money you've deposited as well as the interest it has already accrued. Over time, this can add up to quite a generous sum. Again, there are a variety of options from which to choose:

- *Passbook accounts* can be opened with very little money, but they pay the least interest.
- *Money market accounts* have interest rates that fluctuate with market rates, but sometimes there is a minimum balance that needs to be maintained or a limit as to how much you can withdraw in a given period.
- *Certificates of deposit* are the other kinds of CDs—the ones that offer the highest rates but that tie up your money for an extended period. If you need to withdraw your funds before the CD comes due, you will have to pay a penalty.

- *Individual retirement accounts* (IRAs) are used to put aside money for retirement. However, if you withdraw the funds at an earlier age, there may be a stiff penalty.

As your financial responsibilities increase, you may need more than one savings account. If you are unsure which type of account is right for you, ask a friend or family member whose knowledge you trust or speak with a customer service representative at your financial institution, who will be happy to offer some guidance.

Credit

The keys to the car and a credit card...ah, the great American adolescent dream. As you get older, however, you realize that cars come with responsibilities—maintenance, insurance premiums—and credit cards are not exactly play money. And if you think they are play money, you're bound to get yourself into a game that's way over your head.

Credit is a financial arrangement in which you borrow from a company—Visa, MasterCard, Discover among many—and this gives you the right to defer payment on merchandise or services. In essence, you are using someone else's money to pay for something. But—and this is a big, big but—you must pay back what you borrowed, plus a charge for using the money, called *interest*. So anything you buy on credit will cost you more than if you pay cash.

There are times when using credit is worth the extra price you pay. A genuine emergency like a large medical bill; a genuine necessity like a bed for a new apartment; new tires to get you through the winter...whatever you really, genuinely need badly but don't have the money for right at that moment. On the other hand, going out and buying a pool table or a leather jacket (there it is again!) or a $300 tennis racket just because the credit terms look easy is not such a great idea...particularly when you don't have the resources to be able to pay back the money promptly.

What happens to many people as they accumulate a large balance on a credit card is that they can never do much beyond make the minimum monthly payment, so all they're doing is paying off interest without ever winnowing down the sum that they borrowed. It's another one of those catch-up games that you never quite catch up with.

So be careful when you're using credit. In a really bad situation, where you can't even meet the monthly payment, your creditors can repossess the merchandise you've bought, garnish your salary (which means to take a portion of it until the loan is paid), and wreak havoc with your credit rating; credit will not be available to you in the future when you really want and need it, as when you're looking to secure a mortgage for a home.

The Cost of Credit. Since buying something on credit costs more than paying cash, you need to shop around when you're taking out a loan or applying for a credit card. Different retailers and financial institutions offer different money-lending arrangements, some far more advantageous than others. Be sure to read the fine print, so that you don't wind up paying a prohibitive yearly fee just for the luxury of having a certain card.

When you use credit, make sure you know the *annual percentage rate* (APR), which is the interest that you will be charged per year on the amount you finance. Also, make sure you're well acquainted with the *finance charge*, which is the total of all costs associated with the loan or credit card, be they interest, fees, service charges, insurance, and so on. APRs and finance charges vary widely, so be a smart shopper. And *never* sign a credit card application unless you fully understand its terms.

Credit Cards. Credit cards, popularly known as "plastic," allow you to buy up to a certain dollar amount, called your *credit limit*. This varies widely, depending on the type of card; i.e., silver, gold, or platinum varieties of "plastic." We live increasingly in a "plastic" culture, where the widespread use of credit cards is encouraged for speed and convenience—Internet shopping, for example, is almost exclusively the province of credit card purchases—so consumers today are almost endlessly approached by credit card companies. Among the different kinds of "plastic" are:

- Credit cards, such as Visa and MasterCard, which are issued by banks for private companies such as AT&T. These charge an APR, usually ranging from 16 to 21 percent, and most have some sort of annual fee as well.

- Charge cards, like American Express and Diner's Club, are not as widely accepted as credit cards, except for restaurants and travel. (Some retailers do accept them, however.) The balance on these cards must be paid in full each month or the card will be cancelled.

- Gasoline cards are issued by oil companies and are used to pay for gas and oil at that company's gas stations.

- Retail cards are issued by specific stores, such as Sears, JCPenney or Macy's. They are used to make purchases in those stores exclusively.

Loans. Another type of credit comes in the form of loans. People take out loans for many reasons, such as financing an education (student loans), buying a home (mortgages), fixing up a home (home equity loan), or buying a car (car loan), or a major appliance (installment loans).

When you need to borrow money, you, the borrower, must be seen as a reasonable credit risk. But it's a two-way street. You, the borrower, also needs to be sourcing out a lender with the lowest APR. Some sources of loans are:

- Your relatives, although such loans can come with complicated strings. If you do borrow from relatives, or friends, you'll need to draw up a contract, perhaps sign what is called a *promissory note*, and plan a scrupulous payment schedule. Good friends can become ex-friends when loans are not repaid, and family members are no more likely to look charitably upon chronically outstanding loans.

- Credit unions, if you are a member. These exist to find good financial opportunities for their members, so they are a wise place to start your research.

- Banks and savings institutions. Remember that there is a great deal of variability in this arena.

- Licensed small loan companies, which often charge higher interest because they take on riskier customers.

Whatever you do, make absolutely sure that you steer clear of pawnbrokers and loan sharks. Pawnbrokers lend small amounts, keep your assets, and charge extremely high interest. Loan sharks often operate outside the law and there are no assurances in dealing with them.

Credit Records and Your Rights.
The first time you apply for a credit card or loan, you may be refused because you have no credit record. Then again, you have no credit record because you've been refused credit. How do you get out of this catch-22? Here are several approaches to try:

- Take out a small installment loan—let's say for a refrigerator, if you could use one—and ask someone with a credit record to cosign the loan with you. The cosigner will be responsible for paying in the event that you renege. (We know—you wouldn't dream of it). This is a risk for that person, but if the amount is not too forbidding and the friend is a good one (or the relative a close one), it wouldn't be too presumptuous to ask.

- If you have a savings account with a bank, use it as collateral to borrow money from that same institution. Collateral is property—in this case money—that you give the lender access to as a guarantee that you will pay back the loan.

- Some banks offer credit cards with low credit limits as an introductory offer to students with valid ID cards, or if you have been employed for a year.

- Sign up for utilities in your own name, even if it means paying a large deposit.

- Make sure you pay all your bills *on time*!

The idea behind all this is to get your foot in the credit door and build up a good credit record. These credit records are maintained by companies called *credit bureaus*. Credit bureaus can make clerical mistakes that can be injurious to you, and it is within your legal rights to see your credit record and to know who else has seen it in the previous six months. A small fee is charged for this service. If the information is inaccurate, you can have it investigated and corrected, and copies of the corrected report will be sent to whomever received the incorrect report.

DEALING WITH DEBT

If your debt becomes unmanageable—let's say there are unforeseen circumstances, like the loss of a job, a divorce, or illness—you have a problem you clearly have to deal with. One way that people deal with unmanageable debt is by declaring bankruptcy (more than a million Americans a year file for bankruptcy, in fact). This is a last resort you want to avoid. Before you get to that stage, if you're paying attention, you'll notice some trouble signs. These include:

- Paying only the monthly minimums on your credit cards.
- Skipping some bills to pay others.
- Panicking when you're faced with an unexpected major expense, like a car repair.
- Depending on overtime or moonlighting to pay your basic monthly bills.
- Borrowing from friends and relatives to cover your basic expenses.

If these sound distressingly familiar, you may sense that you're heading for major financial troubles. How can you regain control of the situation? First you have to go through your budgeting process, factoring in your debt and creating a schedule by which you can pay it off. You can try calling various creditors, like credit card companies, to arrange a schedule of payment by which you can absolve your debt. Credit consolidation companies are also available to bring all your debt under one roof and help you develop a schedule to pay off the one sum. Also check out various organizations whose purpose is to help people having financial difficulties. American Consumer Credit Counseling and the National Foundation for Consumer Credit are two organizations that provide credit counseling services, either free or for a nominal sum. These credit counseling firms help people work out long-term debt payment plans and instruct them on how to budget and change their spending habits.

MONEY, MONEY, MONEY...

Money issues never go away. If you don't make money, you have issues. If you make lots of money, you have other issues (admittedly, more pleasant ones). We haven't even touched on a number of financial issues which are going to be very important in your life, like insurance (automobile, health, life), home ownership, and retirement accounts. You'll have to go beyond this book to get an orientation on those matters.

Keep in mind, however, that the best attitude you can have about money is that you're always going to be in some kind of learning curve about it. There's a lot to know about the subject, and nobody expects you to know it all, certainly not now, not yet. But this is as good a time as any to start learning. After all, you haven't got any other choice when you come down to it, do you?

REFERENCE

O'Neill, B. & Wyss, B. (1991, April). Dollars and Sense. *TWA Ambassador*, p. 85.

ROUTE NINE 9

NEVER CHEW GUM ON AN INTERVIEW AND OTHER CAREER THINGS YOU SHOULD KNOW

KEY TERMS

foundation skills
resumé (curriculum vitae)
cover letter

Here you are, busy as can be. You're enrolled in school and perhaps you're working at the same time. If you are working, you may be keeping your eye out for an even better job. If you're not working, you certainly intend to be just as soon as you're qualified to get a job in this industry you've selected. Which brings us to the key word: *selected*.

You've probably worked at other jobs in the past—office jobs, delivery jobs, food service, maintenance—and perhaps those jobs never really satisfied you. But now you're at a new junction in your life when you've gotten yourself together enough to seek out training and to pursue a career in a field that you've *selected*. That means a lot. It proves that you're motivated and that you have a good chance of succeeding at what you've undertaken. You deserve to feel good about yourself for that. And feeling good about yourself may be something you haven't had a lot of experience with in the work area.

Too many people regard work as drudgery—that thing they do five or six days a week, living for those Fridays when they can cast off the constraints of their job and just party, party, party (or else go home, get into bed, and collapse). Surely you agree that it would be a shame to spend so much time involved in something that doesn't offer pleasure or satisfaction. Then there are the lucky people who enjoy themselves so much on the job that it almost feels wrong to call it work. (Yes, such people do exist). In fact, if you recall from an earlier chapter in this book, one of the seven beliefs of highly successful people is that "work is play." Perhaps you wouldn't go quite that far, but at least you should be feeling that "work is good" or "work is satisfying" or that "work is an important part of your life and your identity." If you can't lay claim to any of those feelings, your chances of surviving in any given job are really not very good at all.

We're not trying to frighten you, but the fact is that your time in school is going to fly by and then you will be facing the prospect of finding that job that hopefully will give you the measure of satisfaction you deserve. This then is as good a time as any to start thinking about your career and how you can prepare yourself for it. In this chapter, you will find out how to locate prospective employers and how to present yourself to them. You will learn all about resumés and other employment resources. You will practice filling in application forms and you will be presented with tips for interviewing. You will learn never to chew gum on an interview or smoke or wear huge plastic jewelry or a low-cut blouse or use profanity...in short, a lot of do's and don'ts. So let's get started.

WHAT YOU HAVE TO OFFER

When you're finished with this program in which you're currently enrolled, you will have a certificate that will qualify you to get certain jobs in your field. This certificate, however, does not ensure that you will get a job or even that you really, truly possess the qualifications for a job. The fact that you have met certain criteria to receive this certificate, and have demonstrated a mastery of certain techniques in the field of cosmetology, is only one part of the picture. There is, don't forget, the "whole you," and that is what a prospective employer is going to be looking at.

When you are thinking about finding a job, the way to begin is by looking at yourself and at your personal qualities and foundation skills and to evaluate where you are strong and where you need more work (Figure 9-1).

Personal Qualities	Individual responsibility
	Self-belief
	Self-management
	Sociability
	Integrity
Foundation Skills	**Basic skills:**
	Reading
	Writing
	Arithmetic
	Mathematics
	Speaking
	Listening
	Thinking skills:
	Ability to learn
	Reasoning
	Creative thinking
	Decision making
	Problem solving

FIGURE 9-1 Personal Qualities and Foundation Skills Needed for Solid Job Performance

Source: U.S. Department of Labor, Secretary's Commission on Achieving Necessary Skills (SCANS), *Learning a Living: A Blueprint for Performance*, Washington, D.C., 1992, p. 3.

Looking over this list, it becomes evident that styling hair, as proficient as you may be at it, is not the only skill that a prospective employer will be looking for and it is certainly not the only skill you possess. Ask yourself honestly, which of the above qualities would you say you have? A well-prepared individual, setting out on a career course, should have a good grasp of most of the qualities on this list and the good news is that you probably do. As you successfully make your way through this course, it will become clear to you and those around you that you have a real sense of individual responsibility. Hopefully, this book will prove helpful in boosting your sense of self-belief and self-management. Sociability has never been a problem for you and integrity...well, we're all working on that, aren't we?

Your basic skills—reading, writing, mathematics, speaking, listening—are probably pretty well in place, and as for your thinking skills, such as creative thinking and problem solving, the discussions we've had in this book will hopefully have clued you in to those subject areas as well.

The next set of general skills that the Department of Labor deems necessary for successful job performance are called "workplace skills." These are skills involving the use of resources, interpersonal relationships, information, systems, and technology (Figure 9-2).

Resource Skills	Allocate time, money, materials, space, and staff
Interpersonal Skills	Work on teams
	Teach others
	Serve customers
	Lead
	Negotiate
	Work with people of diverse backgrounds
Information Skills	Acquire and evaluate data
	Organize and maintain files
	Interpret and communicate
	Use computers to process information
System Skills	Understand social, organizational, and technological systems
	Monitor and correct performance
	Design or improve systems
Technology Skills	Select equipment and tools
	Apply technology to specific tasks
	Maintain and troubleshoot equipment

FIGURE 9-2 Workplace Skills Needed for Solid Job Performance
Source: U.S. Department of Labor, Secretary's Commission on Achieving Necessary Skills (SCANS), *Learning a Living: A Blueprint for Performance*, Washington, D.C., 1992, p. 3.

These skills are, obviously, very generalized and will not be required in equal amounts from job to job. In your field, for instance, you should attain a significant level of interpersonal skills, but, while you will have some need for technology skills, it will not equal that of an airline pilot, let's say.

Education and Experience

In addition to the skills and interests listed in the tables on the previous pages, your prospective employer will also be looking to see what kind of education and experience you have had. Your education is not only an indication of what you know—your present course will certify you as having achieved a certain level of mastery in the cosmetology field—but it also indicates what **foundation skills** you have. High school and college degrees imply different levels of foundation skills. The fact that you have completed either or both of those degrees suggests to a prospective employer that you are a person who not only has the ability to learn but that you are someone who can manage yourself and your time and can identify and complete goals, all of which are qualities that employers value.

Your work experience also adds to your value in the eyes of a prospective employer. If you have never worked for real wages, or have only worked part-time, or have been out of the work force for a lengthy period of time, you may be under the impression that you have little to offer in this area. Not so. You need to start thinking of your work experience in a more broadly defined way. Work experience, in addition to full-time paying jobs, can also include:

- part-time or summer jobs
- babysitting, newspaper delivery, yard work
- community or church work
- other volunteer work
- apprenticeships or internships

All of the above represent work situations in which you have exhibited foundation and workplace skills. Employers will understand this and will be receptive when you bring this to their attention.

WHAT DO YOU WANT?

We've talked a little bit about what employers are looking for in potential employees—foundation skills and workplace skills—but keep in mind that the situation here is very much of a two-way street. Getting a loan was a two-way street also, remember? You had to present yourself as a reasonable risk and, at the same time, you were going to shop around for the lender with the best terms. Well, it's important when you're looking for a job to remember that you're a shopper too and a prospective employer has to present a picture that is going to be attractive and promising in order for you to sign on with them.

There are millions of jobs in this country that are waiting to be filled, thanks to the long stretch of healthy economy we've been experiencing. You need to take an inventory of the job criteria that concern you in order to be able to make a decision as to what kind of job you want and what you'd accept. Think of some of the following job criteria when you're making your determination:

- The region of the country where you want to live (Had it with cold weather? Longing for the Sun Belt perhaps?)
- Urban, suburban, or rural lifestyle (Are you hoping to move out of a small town or do you have this dream of moving into one, picket fence and all?)
- Large or small outfit (Do you want to work at a salon in a department store perhaps? Get discounts on store merchandise? In a mall with lots of traffic? Or some exclusive "boutique-type" operation?)
- Job security (Good luck, if you can find it in your field, short of owning your own shop or being in a family enterprise)
- Money (is there a ceiling on how much you can make?)
- Flexibility (Some businesses believe in "flex time," accommodating working mothers and others whose time is compromised by any number of variables. A "worker-friendly" environment is important.)

By making choices in these sorts of areas, you'll be able to focus in on the job you really want. Now the question is: how do you get it?

BEGIN AT THE BEGINNING

You have to realize that when you seriously start to look for a job, you're going to have a lot of work ahead of you. If you do the work well, right from the beginning, chances are your efforts will pay off. Sometimes your job search will pay off in just a few days—you look, you find, presto! you've got a job. In other cases, it can take a period of weeks or even months before you find the right job. And during that period, you're liable to feel a lot of insecurity and even downright fear, so you'll have to come up with some strategies to get you through those difficult times.

When you've been job-hunting for a while and still haven't turned up the right job, you have to keep on motivating yourself. Start out by remembering to give yourself a good dose of that positive self-talk we described at the beginning of this book, and praise yourself for what you've managed to accomplish in the job search process so far.

Boy, doesn't my resumé look beautiful?

I thought I looked like a million bucks today walking into that salon.

People seem to like me. They laugh at my jokes.

Keep up this rewarding, enriching dialogue with yourself as much as you can. There's enough rejection out there in what sometimes seems a cold world and you don't need to add to it by dumping on yourself.

And don't forget the technique of *visualization* that we talked about earlier in the book. When you're going for an interview, it's a good idea to try to actually picture (or *visualize*) yourself in that job. Picture what you're wearing; picture yourself side by side with your co-workers; picture yourself working on a customer's hair. If you keep up with this visualization, you're going to start thinking like someone who already has the job and, next thing you know, you *will* have such a job!

In between all this visualization and positive self-talk, however, there are a number of hands-on tasks that you have to attend to: preparing a resumé, looking for job leads, filling out employment applications, getting references, going on interviews, fielding a job offer and so on. So let's get down to the nitty-gritty.

Preparing a Resumé

Your **resumé** (also known as your **curriculum vitae**, or c.v.) is a short summary of the experiences and qualifications that are relevant to the job you're seeking. Employers often use resumés to screen job applicants—if a resumé comes in with a little smile face sticker on it or a coffee stain or on dayglo green paper, it may go right into the "Out Box." Employers also use resumés as a kind of guide or agenda for the interview, in the event that you're asked to come in for one. Preparing a resumé, although it presents challenges, can also be a highly positive experience for the job applicant, in that it forces the applicant to review past experiences and analyze skills.

Resumés generally contain the following information:

- your name, address, telephone number and, if applicable, e-mail address
- your employment objective
- summary of your qualifications
- education, including school names and locations, dates attended, type of program, highest grade completed, or degree received
- work experience, paid or volunteer. For each job, the job title, name and location of employer, and dates of employment are usually included
- any professional licenses or certificates
- military experience, including branch and length of service, major responsibilities, and special training
- membership in organizations
- special skills, foreign languages, honors, awards, or achievements
- an indication that references are available on request

When it comes to presenting your information on a resumé, you've got two basic formats to choose from. The first, and most common, format is called the *chronological resumé* (Figure 9-3). This approach lists your most recent job first, followed by other jobs you've held, listed in reverse chronological order. Your decision as to whether to present your work experience or your educational experience first on your resumé has to do with the extent of your work experience. If you are a student with little or no work history, you will want to present your educational experience first on a chronological resumé.

Marianne Guilmette
134 Dobson Street
Pittsburgh, Pennsylvania 15219
(412) 555-5489

Objective	A part-time position in marketing
Work Experience	
June 1998 to August 1998	Telemarketer, MDS Marketing Group, Pittsburgh, PA (part-time). Sell magazine subscriptions, books, and videos by telephone.
September 1997 to June 1998	Assistant Manager, Student Store, Noah Central High School (part-time). Responsibilities included selecting and ordering merchandise, advertising, planning and carrying out special promotions, stocking shelves, and helping customers.
Other Related Experience	
November 1996 to Present	Volunteer at Bender Community Center, Pittsburgh, PA Help cook and serve meals to homeless people.
Education	
September 1998 to present	Student, business administration, Pittsburgh Community College.
June 1998	Graduate of Noah Central High School, Pittsburgh, PA Vocational program.
References	Available upon request.

FIGURE 9-3 A chronological resumé

The second basic format for resumés is the *functional resumé* (Figure 9-4). Here the work experience is presented in terms of the functions and skills you have brought to your work. Functional resumés are typically used by people who are changing careers and who want to show that the work they have done previously can translate into their new career goals. They can also be used by people with little or no formal work experience, such as full-time mothers now seeking to enter the work force, because they highlight skills acquired in nontraditional settings. Students with little work experience might also use this format, showing the skills that they've used in school activities and part-time jobs.

WILLIS L. LEMOYNE
67 West Green Street
Greenwood, IN 46143
(317) 555-0935

OBJECTIVE

A position as a CAD drafter/designer in civil engineering.

SKILLS AND ACHIEVEMENTS

- Using CAD system to prepare and revise drawings
- Using plotter and other peripheral devices
- Preparing layout and staking plans from architectural drawings
- Preparing takeoffs for residential and commercial structures
- Working with clients and interpreting their needs
- Developing working designs that meet clients' budgets
- Supporting the sales department as well as the technical engineering staff
- Working under deadline pressure

EMPLOYMENT HISTORY

- Estimator/Drafter, Apple Builders, Inc., Lebanon, IN, 1994-present
- Estimator/Drafter, M&R Construction, Columbus, IN, 1991-1993

EDUCATION

- Associate Degree, Architectural Engineering Technology, ITT Technical Institute, Indianapolis, IN, 1991

FIGURE 9-4 A functional resumé

Whether you use a chronological or functional format, it is important to keep your resumé to just one page. Use action words to describe your skills and responsibilities—*organized, directed, established, prepared*—and use phrases, rather than full sentences, to save space.

An absolute absence of mistakes is essential in a resumé. There must be no grammatical or spelling errors. Have someone or, better yet, several people proofread your resumé for errors. Do not depend on your word processor's grammar and spelling check to catch all your errors (they will not pick up on mistakes like "there car" instead of "their car"). Remember too that certain qualities that play well in a one-on-one situation do not necessarily translate into what plays well in a resumé. Humor, for instance, is a prime example. A good sense of humor may well engage an interviewer, but on the printed page, your attempts at humor may fall flat.

Most important to note is that you must not lie on your resumé. Providing false information, such as saying that you completed a degree when you didn't, is fraudulent and, if you are found out, you could not only lose a job offer but, if you've already gotten the job, you might very well be asked to leave.

Resumé-writing support is widely available through employment agencies, school career centers, and so forth. Check with your school for referrals, if you feel you want to expend the money on such a service.

Finding Job Openings

Now that your resumé is ready to go, you're ready to go. So where *do* you go? To the "Help Wanted" ads? Believe it or not, most jobs are not advertised in the newspaper. If you limit your job search to the Sunday classifieds, you'll only be hitting the tip of the iceberg. Not that it's impossible to get a job out of the "Help Wanted" ads, but you should use as many approaches as you can. Job-hunting is a very active pursuit; you go to jobs, they don't come to you.

Among the sources of information you can use to find out about job openings, in addition to the classified ads, are people you know, employers, school placement offices, private employment agencies, government employment agencies, registers and clearinghouses, and, increasingly, the Internet.

People You Know. Word of mouth is invaluable in terms of finding a job. When you are job-hunting, you need to keep in close touch with your family members, friends, fellow students, instructors, neighbors, and co-workers. Let them know what you're looking for and ask them to keep their ears open for anything that sounds like it might be of interest to you. Don't be shy. Most adults realize that this is an utterly normal part of life. If they do you a favor, you may be able to do one for them sometime (or their spouse or their child or their friend) a favor down the line. In fact, almost half of all successful job-hunters find their jobs through this type of informal networking.

EXERCISE 9-1 Gather Information for Your Resumé

Use the data sheet on the following pages to gather information in preparation for writing your resumé. Make sure you double-check the spellings of all names and the accuracy of dates and addresses. You may not use all this information in your resumé, but it's helpful to have it at the ready in case you need it.

Data Sheet For Your Resumé

Name _____

Address _____

Phone number _____ E-mail _____

Employment Objective _____

Your Qualifications _____

Education

College or Other Postsecondary School _____

Address _____

Date Started _____ Date Ended _____

Years Completed or Degree Received _____ Course of Study _____

Courses Relevant to Employment Objective _____

_____

Honors _____

Extracurricular Activities _____

Work Experience

Job Title _____

Employer's Name and Address _____

Supervisor's Name _____

Date Started _____ Date Ended _____

Description of Responsibilities and Skills Used _____

_____

Job Title _____

Employer's Name and Address _____

Supervisor's Name _____

Date Started _____ Date Ended _____

Description of Responsibilities and Skills Used _____
_____

Job Title _____
Employer's Name and Address _____
Supervisor's Name _____
Date Started _____ Date Ended _____
Description of Responsibilities and Skills Used _____
_____

Professional Licenses

Name/Number of License _____
Licensing Agency _____ Date Issued _____

Military Experience

Rank _____ Branch of Service _____
Date Started _____ Date Ended _____
Description of Responsibilities and Skills Used _____
_____

Special Training _____

Personal Data

Awards, Honors, and Special Achievements _____
_____

Hobbies and Special Interests _____
Foreign Languages _____
Organizations and Offices Held _____
_____

Volunteer Work _____

References (List educational, employment, and character references. No relatives, please.)

Educational Reference

Name and title _____
Address _____ Phone _____

Employment Reference

Name and title _____
Address _____ Phone _____

Character Reference

Name and title _____
Address _____ Phone _____

Employers. You can apply directly to employers even if you haven't heard of any specific job opening there. To find employers that might have positions to meet your job objective, you can:

- look in the Yellow Pages
- check the directories of your local Chamber of Commerce
- consult directories of trade associations at the library
- check the employers' web sites on the Internet

School Placement Offices. Your school should prove helpful in providing job referral services to students and alumni. This is an excellent source of job leads for students, because employers list positions whose qualifications are likely to be matched by students or alumni. Alumni may also turn to their alma mater to find students for positions they are looking to fill.

Classified Ads. Although we mentioned that most jobs are not obtained through classified ads, some people do manage to find a position that way. You'll find employment ads in local newspapers as well as professional and trade publications. Check these every day and if you see something that looks promising, act on it promptly. Some jobs are actually filled even before the ads stop running. Make notations in a record book of which jobs you've responded to and when.

Private Employment Agencies. Private employment agencies can sometimes be helpful, depending on the field and the position you're looking for. There are temporary agencies that you might find useful for some stopgap activity. The thing to remember about private employment agencies, however, is that they exist to make money. Someone will have to pay their fee. If it is the employer, no sweat. If it is you...sweat. Before you decide to use a private employment agency, make sure you read all the fine print on the contractual agreement.

Government Employment Agencies. Turn to your state's employment service for some free help. This service, often called the Job Service, provides free statewide and local job referrals. To find a state employment office, check in your local phone book under your state's Department of Labor or Employment, or visit their web site. If you do visit their office, expect to wait. When something is free, a lot of people tend to turn out for it.

Registers and Clearinghouses. Registers and clearinghouses collect and distribute job information. There are both federal and private clearinghouses, with some specializing in certain fields. Some list employers' vacancies, while others list applicants' qualifications. Some list both. In each case, the cost to the job hunter varies.

Internet Resources. More and more, the Internet is becoming the place to turn to for job opportunities and directions. Corporate web sites often post job openings, school placement offices can usually be reached online, and each day new job fairs open on web sites that are particularly interesting in the sense that they represent a wide geographical area, in case you're open to relocation.

Some of the larger and better-known sites include Online Career Center, the Monster Board, E-Span, the Riley Guide, and Career Mosaic. Also, the U.S. Department of Labor and state employment agencies maintain America's Job Bank, a nationwide database of job listings. When a new job matching your profile comes in, the job bank will e-mail you a notice.

Another way to use the Internet for job-hunting is to post your resumé electronically in a resumé database or a personal home page. Employers can find qualified job candidates by doing key word searches. This may prove less useful than one might hope, however, because it puts you, the job-hunter, in the more passive position.

Writing Cover Letters

A very important component in your job-hunting process is the letter you mail, fax, or e-mail with your resumé. This letter, called your *cover letter*, is designed to seize the attention of whoever sees it, so that it will be passed along to the hiring party and you will be invited in for an interview (Figure 9-5). Therefore, your cover letter needs to be customized; one size does not fit all. You must write a one-page cover letter that is targeted to the particular job you're applying for. Here are some pointers to keep in mind:

- Whenever possible, avoid "Dear Sir" or "Dear Madam" and address your letter to a specific person. This may take some legwork to find out who that person is. You can call the personnel office at the company you're writing to and ask for the spelling of the name and the title of the person to whom you wish to send your letter.

- In the first paragraph, indicate the purpose of your letter; for example, you may be responding to a position advertised in the September 4 *Times-Union*. If you were referred to the company by a specific individual, name that individual in this paragraph.

- In the second paragraph, show how your skills, interests, and experiences qualify you for this job and then refer the reader on to your enclosed resumé for further details.

134 Dobson Street
Pittsburgh, PA 15219
September 12, 1998

Human Resources Manager
TG&B Inc.
P.O. Box 3476
Pittsburgh, PA 15230

Dear Mr. DiNapoli:
I am applying for the position of stylist that you advertised in the September 11 *Pittsburgh Press and Post Gazette*. My resumé is enclosed.

This summer I worked as a stylist for MDS Hair Salon. I was named the Stylist of the Week twice because of high customer satisfaction. Because MDS is moving their location, I am looking for a position in which I can use my cosmetology skills. I think my skills, experience, and motivation will benefit your salon.

I would be happy to come in for an interview. I can be reached at 555-5489 and will call you on September 19 to answer any questions you may have.

Sincerely,

Marianne Guilmette
Marianne Guilmette

Enclosure

FIGURE 9-5 A sample cover letter

- In the third paragraph, request an interview and state where you can be reached. You might also suggest that you will be calling to follow up on your letter.

Again, keep in mind that the cover letter, like your resumé, has to be letter-perfect. Make it positive and upbeat in tone, and keep it all neat and well-organized. If you need help doing this, make sure you get it.

Filling Out Employment Applications

Expect to be asked to fill out an employment application when you call on an employer directly, or before an interview. This form will duplicate much of the information on your resumé, but it is designed for the employer's files. So be sure to bring a copy of your resumé with you when you call on employers, for your easy reference.

When you fill out an employment application, follow directions carefully, write neatly, and do your best with spelling and grammar. If there is a section that does not apply to you—let's say, for instance, "Military Service"—write in a dash (—) or N/A (not applicable) in the space. Do not feel compelled to answer certain questions, as to your age, race, religion, marital status, or arrest record. These questions can be discriminatory and should not be asked by the employer.

Interviewing

One of the most important steps in the job-hunting process is the interview, if you are fortunate enough to be invited in for one. During the interview, you will be asked to evaluate your skills, experience, and character in order to determine whether you are suitable for the job in question. An interview might be very short, depending on the demands on the time of the interviewer, but every moment counts. You have to be sure that you are prepared for each interview, both in terms of presenting yourself in the best possible light and in terms of finding out what you can about the position that is being filled.

Before the Interview. Unless you're a very unusual person, you're more than likely to experience some nervousness before an interview. This nervousness can be kept under control if you undertake a few steps to counteract the tension. These include the following:

- *Do some research about the business.* See what you can find out about this firm from their web site, public relations department, or from word of mouth. Perhaps you'll be able to get some sense of their clientele or what kinds of products they favor. Knowing anything useful like that can help you make a good impression.

- *Be ready to explain why your experience and skills qualify you for this job.* You're selling yourself. Be prepared.

- *Be ready to answer any questions that might come up.* The interviewer may ask you questions like: What are your strengths? What are your weaknesses? Why should we hire you? How much money do you want? Think about questions like these in advance and be ready to discuss them.

- *Be prepared to handle discriminatory questions.* Although employers are not legally allowed to ask certain questions designed to reveal your race, nationality, age, religion, or marital status, sometimes they do. If this happens, you can either answer the question directly, if you so wish and if you feel it does not compromise your chances of getting the position, or you can try to return the interview to its appropriate focus: the requirements for the job. For example, if you are asked how old you are, you might respond with something like, "I am old enough to be certified in my field and to be ready to work."

- *Make sure you are neat and well-groomed and your clothing is appropriate.* Avoid trendy and skimpy clothing, flashy jewelry, gaudy colors, body piercings, excessive makeup, sunglasses, tube tops, sneakers, and the like. Do not wear perfume or aftershave; many people find scent repellent. And NEVER chew gum on an interview! (Need we say that smoking on an interview is just as good as showing up twenty minutes late?)

- *Bring several copies of your resumé, a pen, and a small notebook.* You may want to jot down some notes as you have your meeting.

- *Be prepared to take one or more tests.* You may have to take an aptitude test, a skills test, a medical exam, or a drug test.

- *Know exactly where the interview is and how to get there.* Unless it causes you great inconvenience, rehearse with a dry run sometime before you're actually due there.

- *Plan to get to the interview ten minutes early.* This gives you a chance to use the facilities, collect your thoughts, and cool out a bit. Nothing is as counterproductive as getting to your interview just in the nick of time...or, heaven help us, late!

Getting ready for an interview is very much like getting ready for an exam. The more you prepare, the better you'll do.

The Actual Interview. So there you are, sitting in a room across from this person whom you don't know but who is very central to your getting something you want and need. How do you proceed? How do you conduct yourself?

Remember that trick we talked about called "modeling"? That's when you were with someone you wanted to impress favorably and you would study certain characteristics of that person and reproduce them subtly. Such modeling comes in handy during an interview. Try to adapt to the style of your interviewer. If he is very casual and low-keyed, respond accordingly (this does not mean to put your feet up on his desk, however—or any of your personal belongings!). If the interviewer is very formal, be on your very best behavior. Some interviewers will ask very specific, directed questions and expect short, to-the-point answers. Others talk so much you can hardly get a word in edgewise. Still others just say, "Tell me about yourself," and sit back with folded arms as you rush in to fill the void. You have to be flexible and go with the style of the interviewer.

Again, there are a lot of do's and don'ts to keep in mind when you get into the interview arena:

- Never criticize former employers or complain about them. It does not reflect well on you to do so.
- Do not discuss any of your financial or personal problems. This is an interviewer, not a counselor.
- Avoid controversial topics like politics or religion.
- Don't make up answers that you think the interviewer wants to hear. Keep it honest.
- Listen carefully and be sure you understand each question before you answer. Remember that open-ended questions require more than a "yes" or "no" answer. And keep in mind that it's perfectly acceptable for you to ask the interviewer to further clarify his or her question or for you to take some time before framing your response.
- Be courteous. Make sure you have the interviewer's name right. Do not interrupt him when he's speaking.
- Ask open-ended questions about the firm. In addition to gaining information, you will look interested and intelligent.
- Allow the interviewer to bring up the subject of money. If you are asked what salary you expect, you can turn the question around by indicating that you know the average starting salary in the industry. You can also ask what the company's salary range is. Try not to mention a specific salary first, because you may go too high or too low.

When the interviewer brings the interview to a close, he will probably thank you and tell you that you will be hearing from them. When this happens, it may mean that you have not gotten the job. The interviewer may formally tell you at a later date, by call or letter, that someone else was hired. Do your best not to take this personally. There are many variables that go into an employer's decision to hire someone, and because you have not met them all does not mean that you are an inadequate person.

Another way the interview might end is with your being invited back for a placement or other test or to talk to someone else in the company. If you're asked to take a drug test, find out which types of tests are being used and which foods or medications might trigger a false positive (there have been occasions when a poppyseed bagel will trigger a false positive!). Three-quarters of large and medium-sized firms test for drugs, so to be asked to do so is not an aspersion on your character. When you are invited back, make sure to note the details of your next appointment. Do not rely on your memory, because in the excitement of this promising turn of events, you might be too excited to remember things clearly.

One final way the interview may end is with an actual job offer. If this happens, and you are absolutely, entirely sure that you want the job, then say yes. But, in most circumstances, you should ask for a day to think it over. That way you'll have some extra time to think about the job and the firm and whether you really want to be a part of it.

After the Interview. Whether the interview results in a job offer or not, be sure to send the interviewer a brief letter thanking him or her for his or her time (Figure 9-6).

This kind of courtesy is expected in the workplace, and you never know when your paths might cross again with this very same person. It's a small world, in many ways.

After each interview, you'll also want to do a post-game analysis on yourself. What were your strengths? What were your weaknesses? What might you have said differently? Make each interview into a rehearsal for the next one, not a defeat. Remember that a person often will have dozens of interviews before getting the right job. So you might as well get it right!

---

134 Dobson Street
Pittsburgh, PA 15219
September 12, 1998

Human Resources Manager
TG&B Inc.
P.O. Box 3476
Pittsburgh, PA 15230

Dear Mr. DiNapoli:
Thank you for taking time to speak with me yesterday about the position of stylist at your salon. I was very impressed with your company, and the job sounds wonderful. I'm more convinced that my cosmetology experience can benefit your salon.

Sincerely,
Marianne Guilmette
Marianne Guilmette

FIGURE 9-6 A sample thank you letter

EXERCISE 9-2 Role Playing an Interview

Choose a partner from your class and role play an interview. One of you will be the job-hunter; the other will play the interviewer. Analyze your performance afterwards.

THE LONG HAUL

You may now just be embarking on a career in the cosmetology field. It might be your first job. On the other hand, it might represent a career change for you. Perhaps you've been out of the work force for a long time and this is your way back in. Whatever the circumstances, keep in mind that the average person's working life is a long one—forty or fifty years for many people.

The average person's working life has also become quite varied. Gone for most people are the days when a person worked in the same job for his or her whole life and got a gold watch on retirement. People today are seeing themselves to a greater and greater degree as marketable commodities. They possess a skill and their own compensation and fulfillment is more important than loyalty to "The Company." Similarly, companies don't have the same kind of loyalty to their employees, and downsizing has shattered a great deal of trust for many people.

Goal-setting, which we talked about in the beginning of this book, is an ongoing process. You will be setting goals for yourself and charting your progress all the way through your career. As you gain experience, you may discover that the goals you set for yourself at the start of your career no longer interest you or apply to you. You may find that your work is taking you into new and unexpected directions. Changes in your personal life will also influence your work life. If you are divorced or widowed, you might decide you want to move to another city or even another country, and then, of course, you're changing jobs again, if not careers. You will also find that the world around you is changing so fast that you must struggle to keep up with it. Changes in technology and the global economy affect the way business is conducted, and you mustn't allow yourself to become obsolete. Continuing education and retraining have become a way of life for millions.

The process of self-evaluation and learning that you have begun in this course is an ongoing process. The good news is that, the more you do it, the better you may find yourself getting at it. And the better you get at it, the more likely you are to realize your potential, whatever that may be.

Good luck to you. We wish you well.

NOTES

NOTES

NOTES

NOTES